Better Homes & Gardens.

CHRISTMAS
FROM THE HEART.

Volume 25

Meredith Consumer Marketing
Des Moines, Iowa

CHRISTMAS
FROM THE HEART.

MEREDITH CORPORATION CONSUMER MARKETING
Consumer Marketing Product Director: Heather Sorensen
Consumer Marketing Product Manager: Wendy Merical
Consumer Marketing Billing/Renewal Manager: Tami Beachem
Business Director: Diane Umland
Senior Production Manager: Al Rodruck

WATERBURY PUBLICATIONS, INC.
Contributing Editor: Carol Field Dahlstrom
Contributing Copy Editor: Terri Fredrickson
Contributing Proofreader: Gretchen Kauffman
Contributing Photographer: Jacob Fox

Editorial Director: Lisa Kingsley
Creative Director: Ken Carlson
Associate Editors: Tricia Bergman
Associate Design Director: Doug Samuelson
Production Assistant: Mindy Samuelson

BETTER HOMES AND GARDENS MAGAZINE
Editor in Chief: Stephen Orr
Creative Director: Jennifer D. Madara
Senior Deputy Editor: Nancy Wall Hopkins

MEREDITH PUBLISHING GROUP
President: Tom Harty

MEREDITH CORPORATION
Chairman and Chief Executive Officer: Stephen M. Lacy

In Memoriam: E.T. Meredith III (1933-2003)

All of us at Meredith Consumer Marketing are dedicated to
providing you with information and ideas to enhance your home.
We welcome your comments and suggestions. Write to us at:
Meredith Consumer Marketing, 1716 Locust St., Des Moines, IA 50309-3023.

Contents

TIME TO CELEBRATE!

The merriest time of the year is upon us, and we have a multitude of projects, recipes, and ideas to make your spirit bright. Try your hand at making some felt cookie ornaments that resemble sugar cookies right up to their sugarlike sparkling beads. Let nature inspire you with wood-burned branch slices that become quick-to-make napkin rings or wrap your special gifts with printed papers you make yourself.

Can't get enough Christmas cookies? We love them so much that we have an entire chapter of festive cookie recipes to stir up and enjoy or give as much-appreciated gifts. Try the Black Forest Cookies or the Gingersnap Logs. You'll want to bake them by the dozens! And we have shared some of our favorite slow cooker recipes that will leave you more time to celebrate. Be sure to try the Asiago Cheese Dip and the Greek Stuffed Meatballs—perfect for those holiday parties.

Time running short? No worries! We have dozens of ideas you can make in minutes. You can stitch up colorful felt scarves in less than an hour to give as special gifts. Or try creating quick centerpieces using votive candles, jingle bells, and cranberries.

So get ready to celebrate the very best time of year with handmade projects and homemade treats to make this Christmas one they will cherish forever—a Christmas from the Heart.

Carol Field Dahlstrom

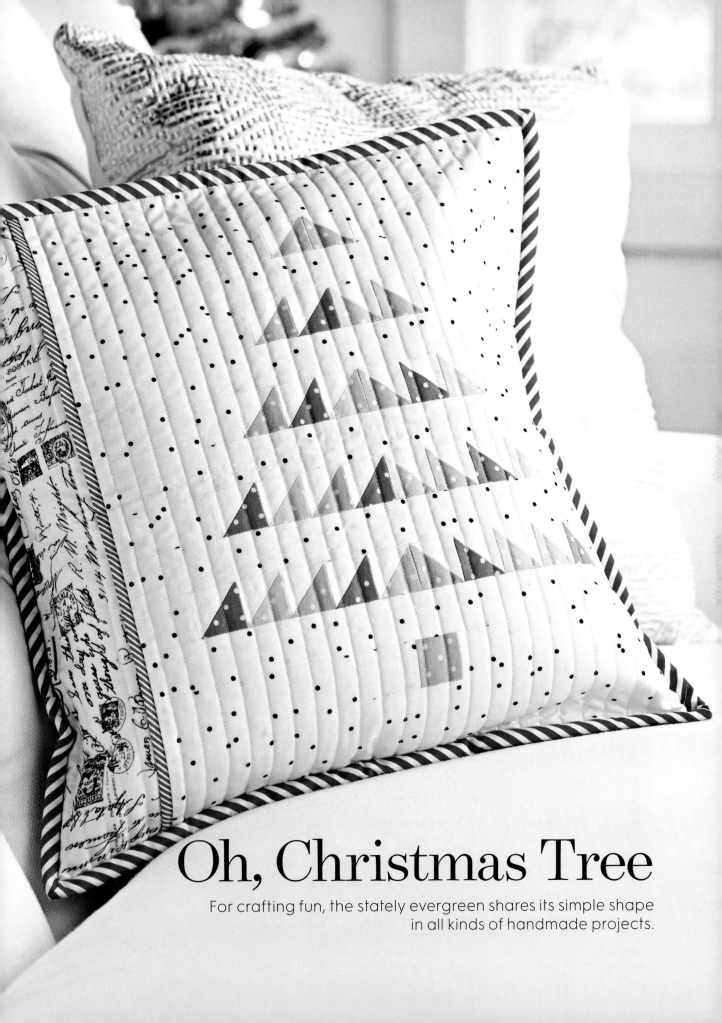

Oh, Christmas Tree

For crafting fun, the stately evergreen shares its simple shape
in all kinds of handmade projects.

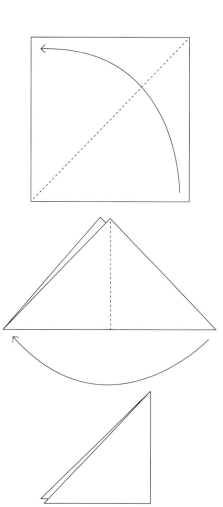

ORIGAMI TREE GREETING CARD

Almost like magic, little bits of paper transform into a lovely little tree to send as a greeting to a special friend.

WHAT YOU NEED

Two 8½×11-inch sheets of white paper • Scrap of gold paper • Scissors • Crafts glue • Purchased blank greeting card in desired color

WHAT YOU DO

1. Cut white paper into ten 3-inch squares. Cut gold paper into a small triangle.

2. Referring to illustration, above, fold squares in half diagonally, touching opposite corners. Then fold the square in half again, touching corners to form a triangle.

3. Plan where the tree is to be positioned on the card. Attach each triangle onto the card with glue, creating the tree shape.

Note: Make sure the fold is in the middle to give the card a 3-D effect.

4. Glue the gold triangle at the top of the tree.

STACKED DOWEL TREE

Stacks of brightly painted dowels stack up to create a clever Christmas tree for holiday decorating.

WHAT YOU NEED

• ⅜-inch-thick wooden dowels, 9 feet total in length • Hand saw • Painters tape • Craft paint in desired colors • Paintbrush • Hot-glue gun and glue sticks • Two 3-inch round wood circles (available at crafts stores) • Small piece of string

WHAT YOU DO

1. Using a hand saw, cut the wooden dowels, three of each length: 2 inches, 3 inches, 4 inches, 5 inches, 6 inches, 7 inches, 8 inches.

2. Tape off each end of the dowels with painters tape and paint with craft paint. Let dry. Remove tape.

3. Glue dowels together using a hot-glue gun, alternating the angle of each dowel. Glue the two wood circles together and glue to the bottom of the tree.

4. Tie a bow with the string and attach to the top of the tree.

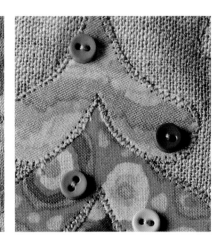

APPLIQUÉ PINE TREE TABLE MAT

Colorful patterned Christmas trees encircle a neutral background to create a perfect table piece to spruce up your holiday table.

WHAT YOU NEED

Finished size is 16-inch circle

18-inch square textured beige linen or 1 fat quarter cotton for background • 1 fat quarter beige print cotton for backing • 1 fat quarter light-medium teal green cotton print for tree branches A and binding • 8-inch square medium teal green cotton print for tree branches B • 6-inch square medium-dark teal green cotton print for tree branches C • 4-inch square dark teal green cotton print for tree trunk • ½ yard paper-backed fusible web • 1 yard stabilizer • 36 (¼-inch) assorted teal buttons if desired for decoration • Green rayon or polyester thread • Beige cotton thread

WHAT YOU DO

PREPARING BACKGROUND AND BINDING

1. Cut and tape the stabilizer together to make a 17-inch square.

2. Following the directions on the circle template on page 14, enlarge and trace the circle. Pin to the wrong side of the background fabric and cut out on the traced line. Replace pins to the right side of the background.

3. Cut the binding fat quarter in half on the diagonal. On this bias cut three 2½-inch strips for binding.

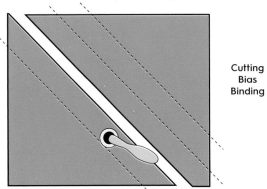

Cutting
Bias
Binding

PREPARING APPLIQUÉ

1. Using the tree appliqué patterns on page 15 and tracing like pieces in groups on paper side of fusible web, trace 8 each tree branches A, B, and tree trunk and 4 tree branches C.

2. Cut excess fusible web from around groups. Fuse according to manufacturer's directions to the corresponding fabrics listed in materials. Cut out each piece on the traced line.

ARRANGING AND STITCHING APPLIQUÉ

1. Remove the paper backing just before arranging the appliqué.

2. Arrange each tree separately on a nonstick pressing sheet. If desired, place the full-size layout under the pressing sheet as a guide. Make four each of Tree 1 and Tree 2.

3. Arrange the trees on the background with the trunks 1 inch from the edge of the circle. Place the four Tree 1 at 12, 3, 6, and 9 on the circle. Place four Tree 2 midway between large trees. Use the original folds on the stabilizer pattern to find the 8 clock segments.

4. Using green thread and a satin or fine zigzag stitch (.85mm long and 1.75mm wide), stitch around the appliqué pieces.

Continued

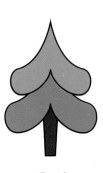

Tree 1

Tree 2

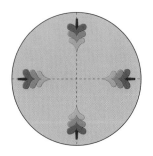
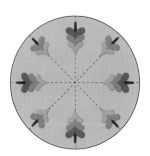

FINISHING

1. Layer the quilt top batting and backing.
2. Quilt as desired.
3. Trim the excess batting and backing to the 16-inch circle.
4. Join the three bias binding strips; fold in half and use to bind quilt.
5. Referring to the photo, page 12, hand-sew or glue on buttons to decorate the trees if desired.

Appliqué Pine Tree Table Mat
16-inch Circle Pattern
Enlarge 150%

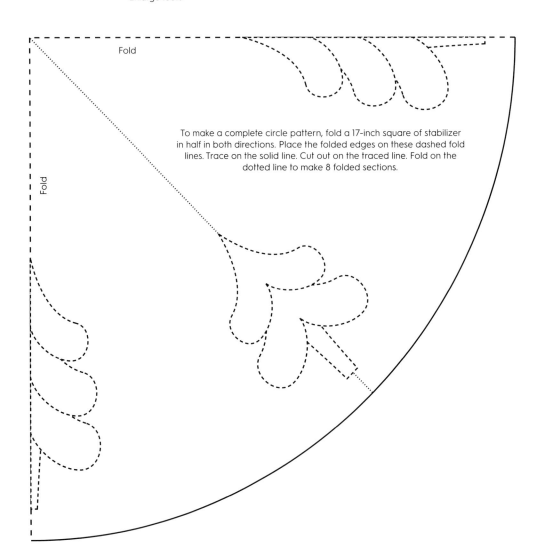

Fold

Fold

To make a complete circle pattern, fold a 17-inch square of stabilizer in half in both directions. Place the folded edges on these dashed fold lines. Trace on the solid line. Cut out on the traced line. Fold on the dotted line to make 8 folded sections.

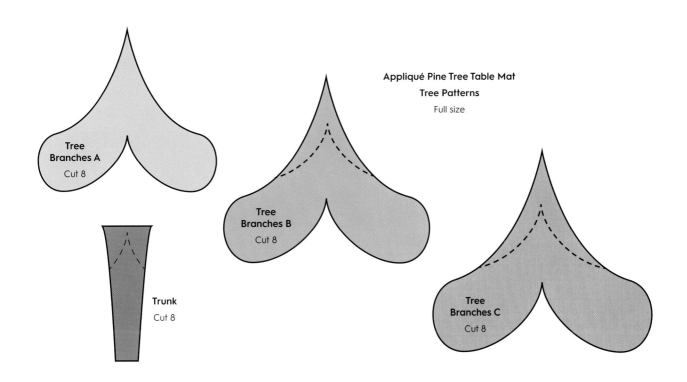

Tree Branches A
Cut 8

Trunk
Cut 8

Appliqué Pine Tree Table Mat
Tree Patterns
Full size

Tree Branches B
Cut 8

Tree Branches C
Cut 8

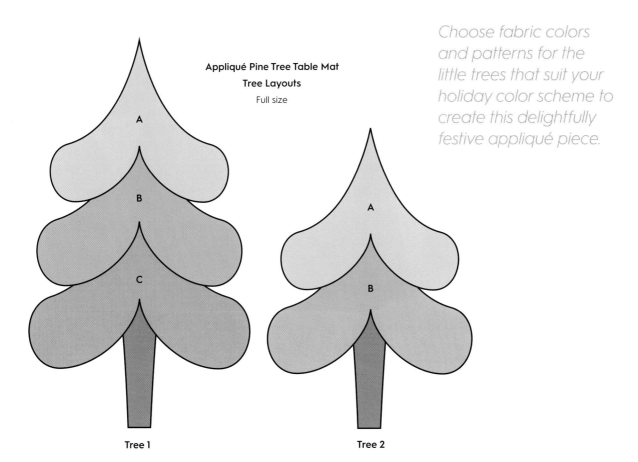

Appliqué Pine Tree Table Mat
Tree Layouts
Full size

Choose fabric colors and patterns for the little trees that suit your holiday color scheme to create this delightfully festive appliqué piece.

A

B

C

Tree 1

A

B

Tree 2

SPARKLING TREE-SHAPED GIFT BOX

Hide a little treasure in this quick-to-make gift box made from cardstock and glittery gold paper.

WHAT YOU NEED

Tree template • Wrap template • 12×12-inch piece of green cardstock • Glitter cardstock • Crafts glue or double-sided tape • Scissors • Scoring tool

WHAT YOU DO

1. Enlarge and copy or trace template patterns, page 17. On green cardstock use the tree template as a guide to trace and cut out tree shape on solid lines. Score paper on dashed lines. Fold and secure with tape or glue.

2. To make the ribbon-style wrap, using the wrap template as a guide, trace and cut out wrap shape on glitter paper. Cut on solid lines and score on dashed lines. Attach with tape or glue around tree shape.

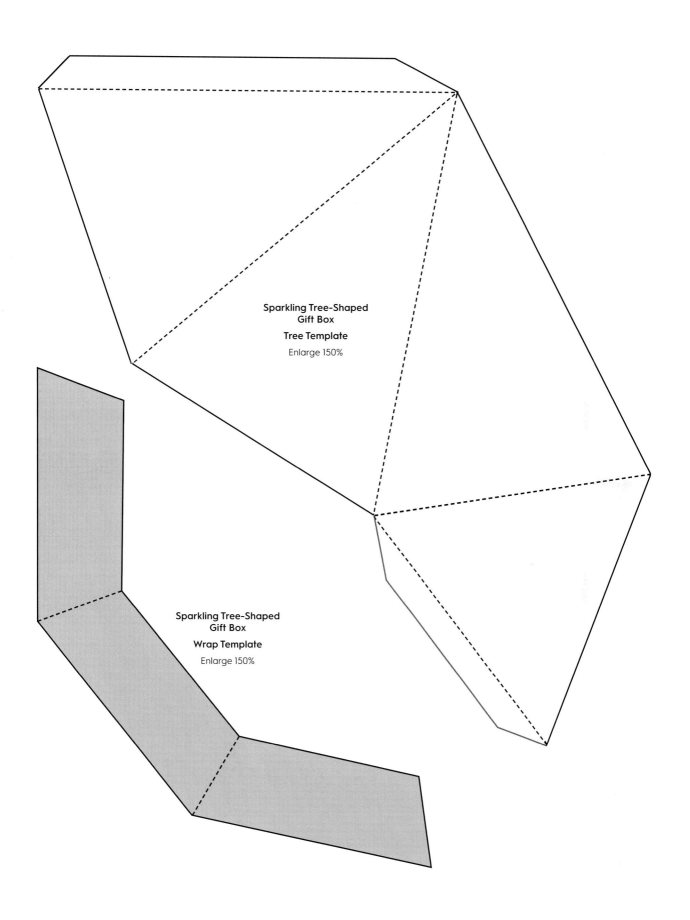

Sparkling Tree-Shaped
Gift Box

Tree Template

Enlarge 150%

Sparkling Tree-Shaped
Gift Box

Wrap Template

Enlarge 150%

Whether using balls of colored felt hanging on strings or mini cedar wreaths lined up on a bright red front door, the familiar Christmas tree shape they make says "Merry Christmas."

FESTIVE FELT BALL TREE

Small felt balls line up to create an illusion of an evergreen tree to hang in your wintry window.

WHAT YOU NEED

41 wool felt balls (39 in shades of green and 2 brown) • Fine string • Needle with eye large enough for string • Ruler • 1-inch square dowel, cut to 10-inch length

WHAT YOU DO

1. Plan the design by laying the balls as they will be strung.
2. Thread the needle with the string. Referring to the photo, left, attach the felt balls to the string by running the needle through the balls (3 green balls, 5 green balls, 7 green balls, 9 green and 2 brown balls, 7 green balls, 5 green balls, 3 green balls). Tie each string around the square wooden dowel, paying attention that the bottoms of the green balls are horizontal and straight and the two brown balls hang below the green balls. Trim string ends.
3. Tie a string around each end of the dowel to create a hanger.

GATHERED-TOGETHER WELCOME

Decorate your front door with a tree shape created from miniature cedar wreaths to greet holiday guests.

WHAT YOU NEED

17 small green wreaths • Small straight sticks • Wire • Wire cutters • Hot-glue gun and glue sticks • 3-inch-wide red satin ribbon

WHAT YOU DO

1. Plan the design of the door decoration by laying the wreaths and sticks on a flat surface.
2. Using the wire, attach the wreaths together to form the tree shape.
3. Hot-glue the sticks together to form a trunk shape. Wire the trunk to the bottom middle wreath.
4. Attach to the door using a wreath hanger, wire, or nails. Make the bow from the ribbon and attach at the top of the door.

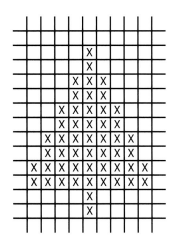

FROSTY TREE KNIT HAT

Children will have fun playing in the snow wearing this tree-motif-inspired knit hat trimmed in winter-white eyelash yarn.

WHAT YOU NEED

1 skein (4 or 5 oz.) green worsted yarn • 1 skein (1 -2 oz.) white eyelash yarn • 5 yards white worsted yarn • Size 8 (5mm) circular needles 16" long (adjust size to obtain correct stitch gauge) • Size 8 double-pointed needles • Stitch markers • Size 16 or 18 tapestry needle

WHAT YOU DO

Gauge: 18 stitches = 4" in stockinette stitch (k 1 row, p 1 row)
Size 2–3 (4—6) years: 18.5" (20.5") head circumference

1. With size 8 circular needles and green worsted, cast on 80 (88) stitches. Join to beginning of row, taking care not to twist stitches. Add place marker (pm).
2. Add white eyelash yarn and purl (p) the two yarns together for 4 rows. Tie off eyelash yarn.
3. Knit every round until hat measures 5" (6") above the eyelash trim rows.
4. On the last row pm every 10 stitches.

SHAPE CROWN:

1. Change to double-pointed needles when the circular needles become difficult to use.
2. Round 1 [sm, k8 (9) to 2 sts before next marker, k2tog] 8 times — 72 (80) sts.
3. Repeat rounds sm and knitting 1 less stitch between markers each round until there is only 1 stitch left between markers — 8 sts.
4. Last round [remove markers as you K2tog] 4 times.
5. Cut yarn, leaving a 12" strand for top of hat. Thread yarn through tapestry needle, weave through remaining sts and pull up tightly, secure. Fasten off.

WEAVE DESIGN:

1. Using the Tree Chart, above left, duplicate-stitch the tree on the front of the knit cap with the white worsted yarn.
2. Start the tree trunk at the center front about 8 rows up from the start of the solid green knitting.
Tip: Choose a circumference size 1 to 2 inches smaller than head measurement.

DUPLICATE STITCHING:

1. Thread a tapestry needle with the white worsted yarn.
2. Insert the needle from the wrong side to the right side at the V base of the first stitch, leaving a 4" tail on the wrong side.
3. Following the line of the stitch, put the needle back in at the top of the stitch, inserting it under the full stitch (V legs) in the row above, bringing the needle back out to the right side.
4. Put the needle back in where you started the stitch at the bottom of the V.
5. Move to the V bottom point of the next stitch and repeat. Weave the tails in the back of the hat.

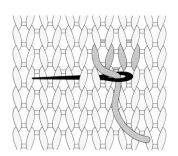

ABBREVIATIONS

k	knit
k2tog	knit 2 together
p	purl
pm	place marker
sm	slip marker
sts	stitches

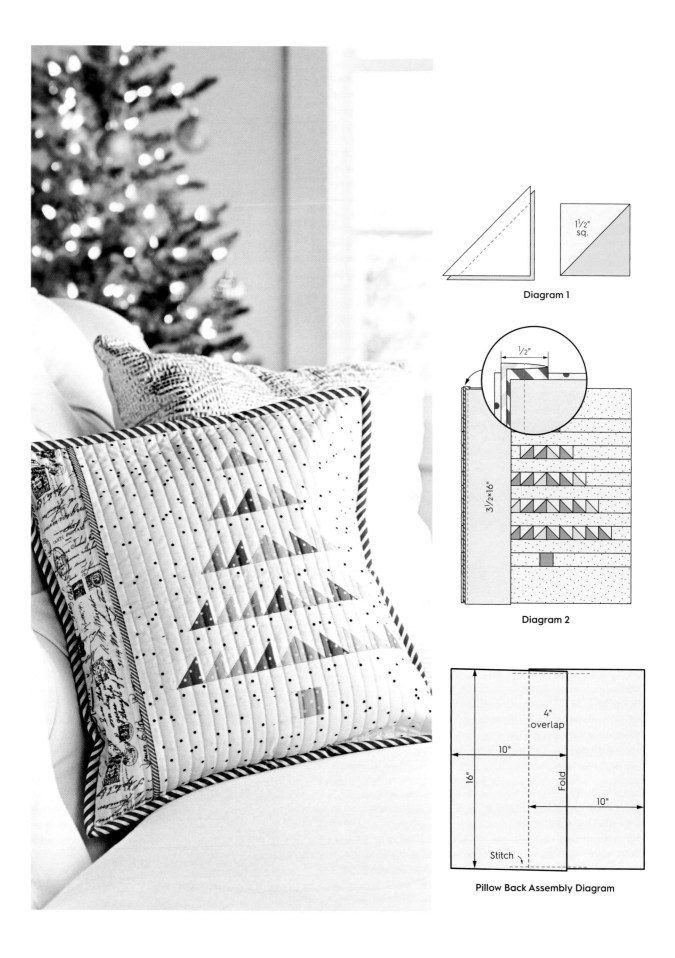

1½"
sq.

Diagram 1

½"

3½×16"

Diagram 2

4"
overlap

10"

Fold

10"

16"

Stitch

Pillow Back Assembly Diagram

PATCHWORK PINE

Dress up a chair or sofa for the holidays with a pretty pieced Christmas tree pillow.

WHAT YOU NEED

½ yard cream-with-black-dot print fabric • ⅛ yard each of light pink dot, dark pink dot, and light green dot fabrics • ⅛ yard of red-and-white narrow stripe fabric • ¼ yard of postal novelty print fabric • 1⅛ yards of backing fabric • ¼ yard of red-and-white wide stripe fabric (binding) • 20-inch square of cotton batting • 16-inch square pillow form

Finished Pillow: 16-inch square
Yardages and cutting instructions are based on 42 inches of usable fabric width. Measurements include ¼-inch seam allowances. Sew with right sides together unless otherwise stated.

WHAT YOU DO

CUT THE PIECES IN THE FOLLOWING ORDER:
From cream-with-black-dot print fabric, cut:
1—3×13-inch strip
1—2½×13-inch strip
15—2⅜-inch squares, cutting each in half diagonally
 for 30 triangles total
5—1½×13-inch strips
2—1½×6¼-inch strips
2—1½×5¾-inch strips
2—1½×4¾-inch strips
2—1½×3¾-inch strips
2—1½×2¾-inch strips
2—1½×1¾-inch strips

FROM EACH LIGHT PINK DOT, DARK PINK DOT, AND LIGHT GREEN DOT FABRIC, CUT:
5—2⅜-inch squares, cutting each in half diagonally for 10 triangles total in each print

FROM LIGHT GREEN DOT FABRIC, CUT:
1—1½-inch square

FROM RED-AND-WHITE NARROW STRIPE FABRIC, CUT:
1—1×16-inch strip

FROM POSTAL NOVELTY PRINT, CUT:
1—3½×16-inch strip

FROM BACKING FABRIC, CUT:
1—20-inch square
2—16×20-inch rectangles

FROM RED-AND-WHITE WIDE STRIPE FABRIC, CUT:
2—2½×42-inch binding strips

ASSEMBLE PILLOW TOP

1. Sew together one cream-with-black-dot print triangle and one light pink dot triangle to make a triangle-square (Diagram 1, page 22). Press seam toward light pink dot triangle. The triangle-square should be a 1½-inch square including seam allowances. Repeat to make 10 light pink dot triangle-squares total.

2. Repeat, using a cream-with-black-dot print triangle with a dark pink dot triangle or a light green dot triangle to make 10 dark pink dot triangle-squares and 10 light green dot triangle-squares.

3. Referring to the Tree Unit Assembly Diagram, lay out the cream-with-black-dot print strips, light pink dot triangle-squares, dark pink dot triangle-squares, light green dot triangle-squares, and light green dot 1½-inch square in rows. Note the orientation of triangle-squares.

4. Sew together pieces in each row. Press seams in one direction. Join rows. Press seams in one direction. The tree unit should be 13×16 inches.

5. Fold 1×16-inch red-and-white narrow stripe strip in half lengthwise with wrong sides together. Pin the strip to left edge of tree unit (Diagram 2, page 22).

6. Sew the 3½×16-inch postal print strip to left edge of tree unit with the red-and-white strip sandwiched between; press seam toward postal print to complete the pillow top.

7. Layer pillow top, 20-inch batting square, and 20-inch backing square; quilt as desired. Pillow top shown was quilted with vertical lines stitched ½ inch apart. Trim pillow top to 16 inches square.

FINISH PILLOW

With wrong sides inside, fold each 16×20-inch backing fabric rectangle in half to form a double-thick 10×16-inch rectangle. Overlap folded edges of rectangles by about 4 inches to make a 16-inch square (Pillow Back Assembly Diagram, page 22). Stitch across overlaps to make pillow back. With wrong sides together, layer pillow top and pillow back; baste. Bind with red-and-white wide stripe binding strips. Insert pillow form through opening in back to complete pillow.

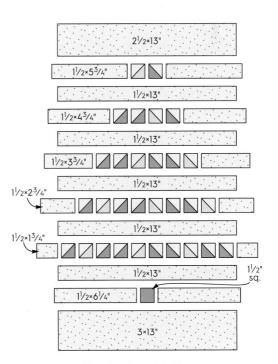

Tree Unit Assembly Diagram

COZY SWEATER TREES

Who doesn't love a warm sweater on a cold, wintry day? This forest of sweater trees repurposes thrift store sweaters and fits perfectly on a mantel, tabletop, or any narrow space. Simply cut tall triangles from cardboard, cover them with sweater pieces, and add burlap-covered cardboard for trunks.

WHAT YOU NEED

Cardboard • Crafts knife • Old sweaters or fabric scraps: red, ivory, green • Hot-glue gun and glue sticks • Scrap of burlap • Ruler • Pencil • Scissors

WHAT YOU DO

CUT FABRICS

1. Use a ruler and pencil to draw tall, skinny triangles on cardboard. The trees shown are 10, 12, 16, and 18 inches tall. Use a crafts knife to cut out the triangles.

2. Lay triangles on flattened sweaters. Cut out sweater pieces 1 inch outside each triangle edge. Apply lines of hot glue over one side of each cardboard triangle and press sweater onto surface; let dry. Apply lines of hot glue on back edges of each cardboard triangle; wrap sweater edges around cardboard and press into glue. Let dry.

3. Cut small rectangles from cardboard for tree trunks. Use cardboard trunks as templates to cut matching rectangles from burlap. Hot-glue burlap pieces to cardboard trunks. Hot-glue top of each trunk to bottom back of each tree.

Classic colors of Christmastime are used in these easy-to-make projects to create colorful mantel trims and ornaments for fun holiday decorating.

DECOUPAGE TREE TRIMS
Tiny bits of colored tissue paper overlap to create Christmas treelike colors on ceramic trims.

WHAT YOU NEED
Ceramic tree shape ornaments (available at crafts stores)
• Small pieces of colored tissue paper in greens, blues, and yellows • Paintbrush • Decoupage medium • Scissors • Fine green glitter • Narrow ribbon for hanging

WHAT YOU DO
1. Place the ornament on a covered surface. Tear or cut the pieces of the paper to desired sizes.
2. Use a paintbrush to paint the decoupage medium onto the surface. Overlap the tissue paper and paint over the top. Continue until all of the ornament is covered. Dust with glitter. Let dry. Thread ribbon in hole for hanging.

Festive
Cookies & Bars

'Tis the season for breaking out the butter, flour, sugar, mixing bowls, and baking pans. You'll find something to satisfy everyone and suit every occasion in this collection of sweets, from tender Eggnog Kringla to no-bake Black Forest Cookies.

SWEDISH VANILLA BUTTER COOKIES

You can substitute an equal amount of vanilla bean paste for the amount of extract called for in a recipe. It's an easy way to get those beautiful specks in your baked goods without cutting and scraping a vanilla bean.

WHAT YOU NEED
- 1 vanilla bean or 1 tsp. vanilla
- 1 cup butter, softened
- ½ cup sugar
- ⅛ tsp. salt
- 2 cups all-purpose flour
- 1 recipe White Chocolate and Vanilla Drizzle

WHAT YOU DO
1. Cut vanilla bean in half lengthwise; using the tip of a knife, scrape seeds into a small bowl; set half the seeds aside for the drizzle.
2. In a medium bowl beat butter with a mixer on medium to high 30 seconds. Add sugar, the remaining vanilla bean seeds, and salt. Beat until combined, scraping bowl as needed. Beat in as much of the flour as you can with the mixer. Stir in any remaining flour. Divide dough in half. Shape each dough half into an 8-inch roll (1¼ to 1½ inches in diameter). Wrap each roll in plastic wrap. Chill 2 hours or until firm enough to slice.
3. Preheat oven to 375°F. Cut rolls into ¼-inch slices. Place 2 inches apart on an ungreased cookie sheet.
4. Bake 6 to 8 minutes or until edges are lightly browned. Cool on cookie sheet 1 minute. Remove; cool on wire racks.
5. Arrange cookies side by side on cookie sheets lined with waxed paper or parchment paper; drizzle cookies with White Chocolate and Vanilla Drizzle. Let stand until drizzle is set. If necessary, chill in the refrigerator 10 minutes. Makes 60 cookies.
White Chocolate and Vanilla Drizzle In a small saucepan heat and stir 4 oz. high-quality white chocolate (with cocoa butter), chopped, and 2 tsp. shortening over low heat until melted and smooth. Stir in the reserved vanilla bean seeds.

EGGNOG KRINGLA

Eggnog and its flavorings—nutmeg, vanilla, and rum—give these traditional cardamom-spiced Scandinavian treats a holiday twist.

WHAT YOU NEED
- ½ cup butter, softened
- ¾ cup sugar
- 1 tsp. baking powder
- 1 tsp. baking soda
- 1 tsp. freshly grated nutmeg or ½ tsp. ground nutmeg
- ¼ tsp. salt
- ¼ tsp. ground cardamom (optional)
- 1 egg
- ½ tsp. vanilla
- ½ tsp. rum extract
- 3 cups all-purpose flour
- ¾ cup dairy eggnog
- 1 recipe Eggnog Icing
  Freshly grated nutmeg or ground nutmeg

WHAT YOU DO
1. In a large bowl beat butter with a mixer on medium to high 30 seconds. Beat in the sugar, scraping sides of bowl occasionally. Beat in the next five ingredients (through optional cardamom) until combined. Beat in egg, vanilla, and rum extract until combined. Alternately add flour and eggnog, beating after each addition until combined. Divide dough in half. Cover and chill 1 to 2 hours or until easy to handle.
2. Preheat oven to 425°F. On a floured surface, roll half of the dough at a time into a 10×5-inch rectangle. Using a sharp knife, cut each rectangle crosswise into twenty 5×½-inch strips. Roll each strip into a 10-inch rope. On an ungreased cookie sheet, shape rope into a loop, crossing rope over itself about 1½ inches from ends. Twist rope at crossing point. Lift ends over loop and the ungreased cookie sheet.
3. Bake 5 minutes or until tops are very lightly browned. Remove; cool on wire racks. Drizzle kringla with Eggnog Icing. If desired, sprinkle with additional nutmeg. Makes 40 cookies.
Eggnog Icing In a bowl stir together 2 cups powdered sugar, ¼ cup dairy eggnog, and ¼ tsp. rum extract until smooth. Stir in additional eggnog, ½ tsp. at a time, to make drizzling consistency.

BLACK FOREST COOKIES

Start with purchased cookies and turn them into a quick take on the Bavarian cake that features rich chocolate and cherry flavors. Kirsch is a German cherry-flavor brandy that can be found at almost any liquor store.

WHAT YOU NEED
¾ cup cherry preserves
1 Tbsp. kirsch (optional)
10 large soft chocolate, chocolate chip, or sugar cookies
1 16-oz. can chocolate frosting
1 Tbsp. kirsch
Maraschino cherries with stem (optional)

WHAT YOU DO
1. In a small bowl combine cherry preserves and, if desired, kirsch. Spread 1 Tbsp. on the top of each cookie.
2. In a medium bowl combine chocolate frosting and Kirsch. Spoon frosting into a decorating bag fitted with a large round tip. Pipe frosting in concentric circles to cover each cookie. If desired, top each cookie with a maraschino cherry. Makes 10 cookies.

GINGERSNAP LOGS

These no-bake treats showcase ground gingersnaps blended with powdered sugar, condensed milk, molasses, vanilla, and cinnamon dipped in a white chocolate coating.

WHAT YOU NEED
1¼ cups crushed gingersnaps
½ cup powdered sugar
⅓ cup sweetened condensed milk
1 Tbsp. molasses or 1½ tsp. rum or coffee liqueur
1½ tsp. vanilla
1 tsp. ground cinnamon
3 oz. white chocolate baking squares with cocoa butter, chopped
1 cup canned vanilla frosting
Red decorative sugar

WHAT YOU DO
1. In a food processor combine 1 cup of the gingersnap crumbs and the next five ingredients (through cinnamon). Cover and process until combined. Transfer to a bowl; stir in remaining gingersnap crumbs. Cover and chill 1 hour or until dough is easy to handle.
2. Line an extra-large baking sheet with waxed paper. Using a rounded teaspoon, shape dough into about thirty-six 1×½-inch logs. Place on prepared baking sheet.
3. In small saucepan cook and stir white chocolate over low heat until chocolate melts. Add frosting; heat and stir until mixture is smooth. Using a fork, dip logs, one at a time, into white chocolate mixture, allowing excess to drip off. Return to waxed paper. Sprinkle logs with red decorative sugar. Let stand 30 minutes or until set. Makes 36 cookies.

You would never guess by looking at—or tasting—these treats that neither requires turning on the oven.

HOMEMADE OATMEAL CREAM PIES

Even the store-bought version of these nostalgic treats is pretty tasty. These homemade sandwich cookies stuffed with marshmallow creme are irresistible.

WHAT YOU NEED
¾   cup all-purpose flour
½   tsp. baking soda
½   tsp. salt
¼   tsp. baking powder
½   cup butter, softened
½   cup peanut butter
½   cup granulated sugar
½   cup packed brown sugar
1   egg
1   tsp. vanilla
1   cup quick-cooking rolled oats
2   tsp. hot water
¼   tsp. salt
1   7-oz. jar marshmallow creme
½   cup shortening
⅓   cup powdered sugar

WHAT YOU DO
1. Preheat oven to 350°F. Grease a cookie sheet; set aside. In a small bowl stir together the first four ingredients (through baking powder). In a large bowl beat butter and peanut butter with a mixer on medium until combined. Beat in granulated sugar and brown sugar until fluffy. Beat in egg and vanilla until combined. Stir in flour mixture and oats just until combined.
2. Drop dough by rounded teaspoon 2 inches apart onto the prepared cookie sheet. Bake 8 to 10 minutes or until edges are lightly browned and centers are set. Cool on cookie sheet 1 minute. Remove; cool on wire racks.
3. For filling, in a medium bowl combine the hot water and the ¼ tsp. salt, stirring until salt is dissolved. Add marshmallow creme, shortening, and powdered sugar. Beat on medium until combined.
4. Spread filling on bottoms of half the cookies. Top with the remaining cookies, bottom sides down. Makes 13 sandwich cookies.

CINNAMON CHIP SNICKERDOODLES

Cinnamon chips, white chocolate chips, and crushed graham crackers (or hazelnuts) dress up these simple cookies for the holidays.

WHAT YOU NEED
2½   cups all-purpose flour
1   tsp. baking soda
½   tsp. salt
½   tsp. baking powder
3   tsp. ground cinnamon
1   cup butter, softened
1¼   cups granulated sugar

½   cup packed brown sugar
2   eggs
1   tsp. vanilla
1   cup cinnamon-flavor baking pieces
1   cup white baking pieces
½   cup coarsely crushed graham crackers (5 squares) or chopped hazelnuts (filberts)

WHAT YOU DO
1. Preheat oven to 350°F. Line baking sheets with parchment paper. In a medium bowl combine the first four ingredients (through baking powder) and 2 tsp. of the cinnamon.
2. In a large bowl beat butter with a mixer on medium to high 30 seconds. Add 1 cup of the granulated sugar and the brown sugar. Beat until combined, scraping sides of bowl occasionally. Beat in eggs and vanilla until combined. Beat in as much of the flour mixture as you can with the mixer. Stir in any remaining flour mixture, the cinnamon pieces, white baking pieces, and graham crackers.
3. In a small bowl combine the remaining sugar and cinnamon.
4. Shape dough into about sixty 1-inch balls. Roll balls in cinnamon-sugar. Place 2 inches apart on prepared baking sheets.
5. Bake 9 to 11 minutes or until bottoms are very lightly browned. Remove; cool on wire racks. Makes 60 cookies.

3. Place 2 Tbsp. sugar in a small bowl. Shape dough into 1½-inch balls. Roll balls in sugar to coat. Place balls 2½ inches apart on an ungreased cookie sheet. Bake 10 minutes or until light brown but still puffed. Do not overbake. Cool on cookie sheet 2 minutes. Remove; cool on wire racks. Makes 24 cookies.

APPLE-CINNAMON STREUSEL BARS

The flavors and textures of a streusel-topped apple pie—ginger, cinnamon, and maple syrup—come together in these quick-to-fix bars filled with cream cheese studded with dried apples and walnuts.

WHAT YOU NEED

2	cups all-purpose flour
1½	cups rolled oats
¾	cup granulated sugar
1	tsp. ground ginger
3	tsp. ground cinnamon
1	cup butter, cut into 8 pieces
1	8-oz. pkg. cream cheese, softened
½	cup finely chopped dried apples
½	cup chopped walnuts, toasted*
½	cup sweetened condensed milk
¼	cup pure maple syrup
1	cup powdered sugar
3	to 4 tsp. milk

WHAT YOU DO

1. Preheat oven to 350°F. For crust, in a large bowl stir together the first four ingredients (through ginger) and 2 tsp. of the cinnamon. Using a pastry blender, cut in butter until mixture resembles coarse crumbs; set aside 1 cup for topping. Press remaining crust mixture firmly into the bottom of a 13×9-inch baking pan.
2. For filling, in a medium bowl beat the next five ingredients (through maple syrup) and remaining 1 tsp. cinnamon with a mixer on medium until well combined. Spread over crust in pan. Sprinkle with reserved topping.
3. Bake 35 to 40 minutes or until top is lightly browned. Cool in pan on a wire rack.
4. For icing, in a small bowl stir together powdered sugar and milk to make drizzling consistency. Drizzle icing over uncut bars. Makes 32 bars.
*Tip To toast nuts, coconut, or seeds, spread them in a shallow baking pan. Bake in a preheated 350° oven 5 to 10 minutes or until fragrant and lightly browned, shaking pan once or twice. Toast small amounts of finely chopped nuts, coconut, or seeds in a dry skillet over medium heat 2 minutes or until fragrant and lightly browned, stirring frequently.

BIG SOFT GINGER COOKIES

These crisp-on-the-outside, tender-on-the-inside cookies are generously spiced and flavored with molasses. Pour a big glass of milk to be sure you have a sip with every bite.

WHAT YOU NEED

2¼	cups all-purpose flour
2	tsp. ground ginger
1	tsp. baking soda
¾	tsp. ground cinnamon
½	tsp. ground cloves
¾	cup butter, softened
1	cup sugar
1	egg
¼	cup mild-flavor molasses
2	Tbsp. sugar

WHAT YOU DO

1. Preheat oven to 350°F. In a medium bowl stir together the first five ingredients (through cloves).
2. In a large bowl beat butter with a mixer on medium to high 30 seconds. Add 1 cup sugar. Beat until combined, scraping bowl occasionally. Beat in egg and molasses until combined. Beat in as much of the flour mixture as you can with the mixer. Stir in any remaining flour mixture.

SALTED CHEWY CARAMEL BARS

These intense bars have something for everyone—caramel, chocolate, nuts, and a sprinkle of sea salt atop a crunchy pretzel crust. Yum!

WHAT YOU NEED

1   cup butter, softened
1   cup granulated sugar
1   cup packed brown sugar
2   eggs
1½   cups all-purpose flour
1   cup finely crushed pretzels
½   tsp. salt
1   tsp. baking soda
3   cups rolled oats
1   14-oz. can sweetened condensed milk
1   11-oz. pkg. premium caramel bits
2   tsp. vanilla
1   cup milk chocolate pieces
1   cup chopped salted cashews
¼   tsp. sea salt

WHAT YOU DO

1. Preheat oven to 350°F. Line a 15×10-inch baking pan with foil, extending foil over pan edges.
2. In a large bowl beat butter with a mixer on medium to high 30 seconds. Add granulated and brown sugars. Beat until combined and fluffy, scraping sides of bowl occasionally. Beat in eggs until combined. In a bowl combine flour, pretzels, the ½ tsp. salt, and baking soda. Gradually beat flour mixture into butter mixture. Stir in oats; set aside 1 cup. Press remaining oat mixture into the prepared pan.
3. In a medium saucepan combine sweetened condensed milk and caramel bits. Heat and stir over medium-low heat until caramel melts and mixture is smooth. Remove from heat. Stir in vanilla. Pour caramel over oat crust in pan. Sprinkle with chocolate pieces, cashews, sea salt, and the remaining oat mixture.
4. Bake 20 to 25 minutes or until top is lightly browned. Remove; cool on wire rack. Use the edges of foil to lift uncut bars out of pan. Cut into bars. Makes 60 bars.

BUTTERSCOTCH BITES

A crust based on crushed chocolate wafers and a filling that starts with a package of instant pudding or pie filling mix makes quick work of these bars. Just allow at least 2 hours of chilling time before serving.

WHAT YOU NEED

1½   cups powdered sugar
1   cup creamy peanut butter
6   Tbsp. butter, melted
1   9-oz. pkg. chocolate wafers, crushed
⅓   cup milk
3   Tbsp. butterscotch or cheesecake instant pudding and pie filling mix
¾   cup butter, softened

½   tsp. vanilla
3½   cups powdered sugar
½   cup butterscotch-flavor pieces
1   tsp. shortening

WHAT YOU DO

1. Line a 13×9-inch pan with foil, extending foil over edges of pan. For crust, in a large bowl stir together the 1½ cups powdered sugar, peanut butter, and the 6 Tbsp. melted butter. Stir in crushed chocolate wafers. Press mixture into the bottom of prepared pan. Chill while preparing middle layer.
2. For the middle layer, in a small bowl combine milk and pudding mix. In a large bowl beat the ¾ cup softened butter with a mixer on medium to high 30 seconds. Beat in pudding mixture and vanilla. Gradually beat in the 3½ cups powdered sugar until smooth and spreadable. Spread over chilled crust.
3. In a microwave-safe bowl combine butterscotch pieces and shortening. Microwave on high 1 minute or until melted, stirring every 30 seconds. Pour into a heavy resealable bag; snip a small hole in one corner of bag. Drizzle in a crisscross pattern over bars in pan.
4. Cover and chill at least 2 hours. Using the edges of the foil, lift uncut bars out of pan. Cut into bars. Makes 40 bars.

FOUR-LAYER NOUGAT BARS

Like chocolate bars infused with crisped rice? Try these bars with layers of chocolate and butterscotch, nut-studded nougat, caramel, and a peanut-butter flavor topping all over crunchy base.

WHAT YOU NEED
1   12-oz. pkg. semisweet chocolate pieces
1¼ cups butterscotch-flavor pieces
2   cups crisp rice cereal
1¼ cups sugar
⅓   cup butter
1   5-oz. can evaporated milk
1   7-oz. jar marshmallow creme
½   cup creamy peanut butter
1¾ cups cocktail peanuts or salted cashews, chopped
1   14-oz. pkg. vanilla caramels, unwrapped

WHAT YOU DO
1. Line a 15×10-inch baking pan with foil, extending the foil over edges of the pan. Lightly grease foil.
2. In a medium saucepan combine chocolate pieces and 1 cup of the butterscotch pieces. Cook and stir over medium-low heat until melted. Transfer half to a small saucepan.
3. For the base, stir rice cereal into chocolate mixture; immediately pour into prepared pan and spread to edges. Press firmly. Place pan in freezer while preparing nougat layer.
4. For the nougat, in a medium saucepan combine sugar, butter, and ½ cup of the evaporated milk. Bring to boiling over medium-high heat; reduce heat to medium. Simmer 5 minutes. Add remaining ¼ cup butterscotch pieces; stir until melted.

Remove from heat. Stir in marshmallow creme and ¼ cup of the peanut butter. Stir in chopped peanuts. Pour nougat over chilled base layer in pan; spread to edges. Return pan to freezer while preparing caramel layer.
5. For caramel layer, in a large microwave-safe bowl combine caramels and the remaining evaporated milk. Microwave on high 2 minutes or until caramels are melted, stirring every 30 seconds. Pour over chilled nougat layer; spread to edges. Return pan to freezer while preparing top layer.
6. Add the remaining ¼ cup peanut butter to the reserved chocolate-butterscotch mixture in the small saucepan. Heat and stir over medium-low heat until smooth. Pour over caramel layer; spread to edges.
7. If desired, sprinkle with additional chopped peanuts. Cover and chill bars 2 hours. Using the edges of the foil, lift uncut bars out of pan. Cut into bars. Makes 60 bars.

PISTACHIO BARS

These treats are as much candy as they are bars. Look for unsalted roasted pistachio nuts for the topping.

WHAT YOU NEED
1   egg, lightly beaten
½   cup butter
¼   cup unsweetened cocoa powder
2   Tbsp. granulated sugar
1   tsp. vanilla
2   cups finely crushed cinnamon graham crackers
½   cup finely chopped pistachio nuts
¼   cup butter, softened
¼   cup pistachio instant pudding and pie filling mix
¼   cup half-and-half, light cream, or milk
1½   cups powdered sugar
6   oz. bittersweet chocolate, coarsely chopped
¼   cup butter
½   cup coarsely chopped pistachio nuts

WHAT YOU DO
1. Line a 9×9-inch baking pan with foil, extending the foil over edges of pan.
2. In a medium saucepan combine the first five ingredients (through vanilla). Cook and stir over medium-low heat until butter is melted and mixture just starts to bubble. Remove from heat. Stir in crushed graham crackers and the finely chopped pistachios. Press crumb mixture onto the bottom of the prepared pan.
3. For filling, in a medium bowl beat the ¼ cup softened butter, the dry pudding mix, and half-and-half with a mixer on medium until combined. Gradually add powdered sugar, beating well. Carefully spread filling over crust in pan. Cover and chill 1 hour or until firm.
4. For topping, in a small saucepan cook and stir chocolate and the ¼ cup butter over low heat until melted. Spread topping over filling. Sprinkle with the coarsely chopped pistachios. Cover and chill 2 hours or until firm. Using the edges of the foil, lift uncut bars out of pan. Cut into bars. Makes 25 bars.

Joyful Jars

Functional, frugal, and fun, these dressed-up jars will add a touch of sparkle and whimsy to your holiday decorating.

Clear canning jars are transformed into festive decorations with sparkling lights. Unexpected embellishments such as drawer pulls and patterned paper tape dress up jars for simple gift giving.

SILVER AND SPARKLE JAR

Bursts of sparkling light showcase shiny silver balls in this clever jar decoration.

WHAT YOU NEED

Wide-mouth clear quart canning jar with flat and lid • Battery-operated lights • Small silver ball ornaments • Silver scrapbook paper • Scissors • Silver ribbon

WHAT YOU DO

1. Be sure the jar is clean and dry.
2. Tuck the lights and the ornaments into the jar, arranging as desired. Turn on the lights.
3. Using the jar flat as a pattern, draw a circle onto the silver paper. Cut out.
4. Place the jar flat and paper on top of the jar and then screw top onto the jar. Tie a ribbon around the jar.

FESTIVE JAR DISPLAY

Drawer knobs in all shapes and sizes become colorful toppers for jars of sweet treats that share a painted drawer.

WHAT YOU NEED

3 clear pint jars with flats and lids • Awl • 3 drawer knobs in desired colors and styles • Paper tape such as washi tape • Scrapbook paper in desired pattern and color • Scissors • Candy • Drawer or box • Fresh greenery

WHAT YOU DO

1. Be sure the jars are clean and dry.
2. Using an awl, make a hole in the middle of each jar flat.
3. Using the jar flat as a pattern, draw a circle onto scrapbook paper for each lid. Cut out. Make a hole in the center of the paper to align with the hole in the jar flat.
4. Unscrew the back of the knob. Place the jar flat, paper, and then drawer knob through the hole and tighten with back of knob. Repeat for each topper.
5. Fill the jar with candy or treats. Place the flat with paper and knob on top. Screw on the screw top.
6. Use paper tape to decorate around the top of the jar.
7. Arrange the three jars in a painted box or drawer and add fresh greenery.

PEPPERMINT JARS

Little blue jars are wrapped with red-and-white bakers twine and adorned with silver charms to make quick gifts for friends and family.

WHAT YOU NEED

Half-pint jars with flats and lids • Red-and-white bakers twine • Crafts glue • Paintbrush • Pink scrapbook paper • Small peppermint candies or other small items • Scissors • Small silver charms

WHAT YOU DO

1. Be sure the jars are clean and dry.

2. Starting at the bottom edge of the jar, apply a small amount of crafts glue using a paintbrush. Adhere the bakers twine and begin wrapping the jar, adding glue right before wrapping the twine. End about halfway up the jar, securing with glue. Let dry.

3. Using the jar flat as a pattern, draw a circle onto the pink paper. Cut out.

4. Fill the jar. Place the jar flat and paper on top and then screw the top onto the jar.

5. Thread the charms onto the twine and tie around the jar.

HOMEMADE JAR CANDLES

Choose the color that suits your style and then make colorful candle jars for holiday decorating.

WHAT YOU NEED

Half-pint short jars • Old candles in desired color • Hammer and screwdriver • Empty can to fit into pan • Old pan • Water • Heat source such as hot plate or stove • Candle wicking • Bamboo sticks • String

WHAT YOU DO

1. Be sure the jars are clean and dry.

2. Prepare to melt the wax. On a flat surface such as a sidewalk, carefully use the hammer and screwdriver to break up the old wax. Place in the empty can.

3. Place the wax in the can into the old pan (Photo 1). Place about 3 inches of water around the can. Place on heat source and heat water. Watch carefully and heat only until wax is melted. Remove from heat. **Note:** Heating wax can be dangerous and can explode if it gets too hot.

4. Carefully pour the wax into the jars. Place a cut piece of candle wicking into each jar and wrap the top around the bamboo stick to secure (Photo 2). Cool until set. Remove bamboo sticks and trim wicks.

5. Wrap a string around the top of the jar and tie a knot.

Never leave a burning candle unattended.

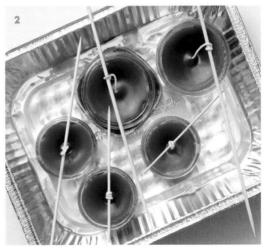

VINTAGE DISPLAY JARS

Showcase one-of-a-kind holiday figurines inside ordinary glass jars for an extraordinary look.

WHAT YOU NEED

Clear canning jars with lids • Small holiday figurines to fit in jars • Double-stick tape • Small items like pieces of tinsel or small ornaments

WHAT YOU DO

1. Be sure the jars are clean and dry.
2. Remove the lid or flat and use double-stick tape to secure the items on the inside of the flat.
3. Screw the jar onto the lid while keeping the jar upside down.

WINTER-WONDERFUL JAR VASES
*Painted jars decorated with winter snowflakes make
beautiful vases for your favorite holiday flowers.*

WHAT YOU NEED
Clear glass jar in desired size • White and light blue chalk
paint suitable for glass • Paint brush • Purchased white
snowflake stickers • Flowers

WHAT YOU DO
1. Be sure the jars are clean and dry.
2. Following the manufacturer's instructions, paint the inside of
the jar with the chalk paint. Allow to dry and cure as directed.
3. Adhere the snowflake stickers to the jars.
4. Fill with water and add blooms.

Pint-size jars filled with water float fresh cranberries and oranges for a fragrant holiday centerpiece. Tiny jars filled with candy become take-aways for each guest at your holiday table.

CRANBERRY CANDLE JARS

Simple and sweet, these floating candle jars can be created in the blink of an eye!

WHAT YOU NEED

Wide-mouth pint jars • Orange ribbon • Fresh cranberries • Dried orange slices • Bits of greenery • Wire • Wire cutters • Water • Floating candles • Scissors

WHAT YOU DO

1. Be sure the jars are clean and dry.
2. Wrap the ribbon around the jar top and tie. Poke the cranberries and orange slices with a piece of wire and tie around the top of the jar, adding a little piece of greenery under the ribbon.
3. Fill the jar with water and add the candles and fruit.
4. Trim the ends of the ribbon as needed.

PERSONAL PLACEHOLDERS

Share a sweet take-home jar for each guest by filling little jars with candy and embellishing with felt fabric holly.

WHAT YOU NEED

Small short canning jars with flats and lids • Neutral color cardstock • Small hole punch • Bakers twine • Marker • Green felt • Red pom-poms • Hot-glue gun and glue sticks

WHAT YOU DO

1. Be sure the jars are clean and dry.
2. Write guests' names on small pieces of cardstock or paper using a marker. Punch holes in each side to attach to jar with twine. Wrap around the jar and tie in the back.
3. Using the template on page 49 as a guide, cut 2 leaves from green felt. Using a glue gun, attach felt leaves and red pom-poms for holly to the jar.
4. Using the jar flat as a pattern, trace around a piece of green felt. Fill the jar with candy; add the jar flat and felt. Screw on the lid.

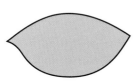

**Personal Placeholders
Leaf Template**

PRETTY PAPER-TOPPED JARS

Folded scrapbook papers turn humble quilted jelly jars into sparkling little giveaways.

WHAT YOU NEED

Quilted jelly-size jars with flats and lids • Light- to medium-weight scrapbook paper with snowflake design • Crafts glue • Fine blue glitter • Scissors • Double-stick tape • Paper tape such as washi tape

WHAT YOU DO

1. Be sure the jars are clean and dry.

2. Enlarge if necessary, and trace or copy the templates, right, and cut out. Trace onto scrapbook paper. Fold the template on the dotted lines and bring together to make a medallion. Use crafts glue or double-stick tape to secure. Glue the circle to the top of the folded medallion. Let dry. Run a line of glue around the edges of the medallion and the circle and dust with glitter.

3. Fill the jar with candies or gifts. Place the flat on the top, screw on the lid, and adhere the medallion with double-stick tape.

4. Use paper tape to trim the edges of the lid.

WINTER WHITE LUMINARIAS

Creamy white jar luminarias light up the night. Using clear jars, doilies, white rice, and string, you can make these by the dozens.

WHAT YOU NEED

Clear pint canning jars • White paper doilies • Decoupage medium • Scissors • Paintbrush • Wet cloth • String • White rice • White votive candle

WHAT YOU DO

1. Be sure the jars are clean and dry.

2. Plan the design by cutting the doilies, leaving a curved edge. Clip the edges and decoupage to the top of the jar, clipping and painting on the decoupage medium. Wipe off any excess using a wet cloth. Let dry.

3. Wrap the string around the top of the jar and tie.

4. Fill the jar one-third full of rice. Put candle in rice.

Never leave a burning candle unattended.

STICKER JARS

Simple stickers reflect the contents of these sweet jars that make quick and easy gifts.

WHAT YOU NEED

Clear pint canning jars • Stickers that match the contents of the jar • Objects that go into jars such as gingerbread cookies, candy canes, ornaments, etc. • Bakers twine • Scissors

WHAT YOU DO

1. Be sure the jars are clean and dry.

2. Affix the stickers to the jars. Fill the jars with chosen items.

3. Wrap twine around the tops of the jars and trim ends.

Pretty Paper-Topped Jars Template

Enlarge 150%

Fold on dotted lines.

Pretty Paper-Topped Jars Medallion Top

Full-size pattern

Making the Rounds

Lovely wreaths using fresh evergreens or unexpected materials are showcased in this chapter of welcoming wreaths for your holiday home.

FELTED FLOWER WREATH

Soft colors in nonwoven felt transform into beautiful blooms to embellish a wreath made of natural driftwood.

WHAT YOU NEED

12-inch plastic wreath form • Driftwood pieces (available at crafts stores) • Hot-glue gun and glue sticks • Nonwoven felt such as National Nonwovens Butter cream 0404, Wheatfields 2610, Grassy meadows 2710, Moss 0730, Grandma's Garnet 0986, Pretty in Pink 2211, or desired colors • Scissors • Small red pom-poms• Small pieces of greenery • Green and gray grosgrain ribbon

WHAT YOU DO

1. Plan the placement of the driftwood pieces and attach the pieces around the wreath form using a hot-glue gun and glue sticks. Set aside.

CREATE THE FLOWERS:

2. For the Poinsettia: Using the templates, below, cut 5 petals from the Poinsettia Small and 5 petals from the Poinsettia Large templates. To form the bottom layer, attach 5 Poinsettia Large petals together in a circle using a hot-glue gun. On the remaining 5 Poinsettia Small petals, cinch the tip of each petal, securing with a dab of hot glue. Then arrange the petals and attach on top of the first layer. Hot-glue pom-poms to center.
3. For the Basic Flower: Using the template, cut 10 petals. Attach them together in two layers of 5 each using a glue gun. Attach a Flower Center.
4. For the Small Flower: Cut two 2-inch circles. Fold in half, securing with hot glue. When dry, fold in half again, securing with hot glue. Do this to both circles, then glue circles together.
5. For the Flower Center: Cut a strip of felt about ¾×4-inches. Cut slits every ¼ inch in the felt, being careful not to cut all the way through, Roll the strip from one end; use a glue gun to attach to flower.
6. For the Leaf: Use the Poinsettia Large and Poinsettia Small templates to create leaves using green felt.
7. Hot-glue the felt flowers onto the driftwood wreath as desired. Add small sprigs of greenery around the flowers.
8. Layer the ribbons and loop around the top for hanging.

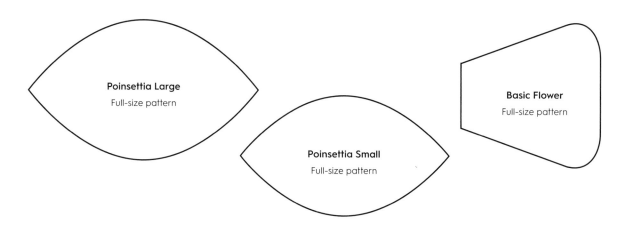

Poinsettia Large
Full-size pattern

Poinsettia Small
Full-size pattern

Basic Flower
Full-size pattern

GOLDEN GLOW WREATH

Gold walnut "nuggets" are spray-painted and tucked into pinecones for a sparkling holiday wreath.

WHAT YOU NEED

Painted or natural pinecones • Florists wire • Wire cutters • 12-inch wire wreath form • Small gold ornaments • Walnuts in the shell • Metallic gold spray paint • 2-inch-wide gold ribbon • Scissors

WHAT YOU DO

1. Plan the arrangement of the pinecones on the wreath. If desired, paint the pinecones first by spray-painting them. Wire the pinecones onto the wreath.
2. Spray-paint the walnuts gold. Let dry.
3. Wire the gold ornaments and gold walnuts onto the wreath on top of or between the pinecones.
4. Loop the ribbon around the wreath for hanging.

SPARKLING ORANGE-SLICE WREATH

Fresh oranges are sliced, dried, and then glittered to create a citrusy-sweet wreath.

WHAT YOU NEED

4 or 5 medium-size oranges • Sharp knife • Hydrogen peroxide • Small bowl • Paper towels • Cookie sheet • Foil • Oven • 12-inch flat foam wreath form • 3 yards of 1-inch-wide burlap ribbon • Hot-glue gun and glue sticks • Scissors • Florists wire • Wire cutters • Crafts glue • Copper-color glitter • 3 jingle bells in metallic colors • Shiny orange ribbon • Small pieces of greenery

WHAT YOU DO

1. Slice the oranges very thin using the knife. Pour the hydrogen peroxide into the small bowl. Dip the orange slices into the liquid. Lay the oranges on the paper towels to dry overnight.
2. Cover the cookie sheet with foil. Lay the oranges on the cookie sheet. Place in a 250°F oven for about an hour, turning once. Dry in oven until oranges look and feel dry.
3. Remove from oven and let dry overnight.
4. Wrap the wreath form with the burlap ribbon. Hot-glue ends in place. Hot-glue the oranges onto the wreath, overlapping as desired.
5. Use crafts glue to add glitter to the edges of the orange slices.
6. Wire the bells to the top of the wreath. Loop a ribbon around for hanging. Tuck in greenery.

CHARMING CROP

Create a wreath that pays homage to the harvest and the holidays by showcasing vivid red berries, barley seed heads, and tufts of wheat arranged in symmetrical circles.

WHAT YOU NEED

12-inch-diameter boxwood wreath form • Fresh or faux winterberry, marsh berry, or high-bush cranberry clusters • 1 bundle dried barley • 1 bundle dried wheat • 1 cup fake snow • Hot-glue gun and glue sticks

WHAT YOU DO

1. Glue berry clusters in a 2-inch-wide band around the center of the wreath. Glue barley stems around the wreath's inner edge, layering the tips counterclockwise and facing the same direction.

2. Glue wheat tips in the same fashion along the wreath's outer edge. Let dry. Hang the wreath and dust it with fake snow. (Set a towel on the floor below the wreath to catch surplus flakes.)

AT FIRST BLUSH

Present common Christmas colors in unexpected ways by using dried red dahlias, shiny berries, and lotus pods with chartreuse greenery and yellow berries to make a glorious wreath.

WHAT YOU NEED

14-inch-diameter evergreen wreath form • 3 red lotus pods • 3 dried red dahlias • Preserved burning bush leaf sprigs • Pepper berry leaves • Pepper berries • Yellow berries • Evergreen tips • 1 cup fake snow • Hot-glue gun and glue sticks

WHAT YOU DO

1. Position pairs of lotus pods and dahlias on the wreath and glue in place. Let dry. Tuck leaf sprigs, berry leaves, berries, and evergreen tips around the pods and flowers, gluing them in place as needed.

2. Continue adding materials until the wreath looks pleasantly plush. Hang the wreath and dust it with fake snow. (Set a towel on the floor below the wreath to catch surplus flakes.)

Your guests are sure to smile when they see a chrome-inspired vintage wreath that decorates the grille of a special classic car that sits in the driveway.

CHARMING VINTAGE WREATH

Chrome-color pinecones, vintage tinsel, and painted silver sticks add charm to this fresh evergreen wreath that adorns a classic car.

WHAT YOU NEED

Fresh evergreen wreath • Pinecones • Chrome spray paint • Small sticks • Silver vintage-style tinsel • 3 yards of 3-inch-wide red and silver ribbon • Florists wire • Wire cutters • Scissors • Small red and silver nonbreakable ornaments • Silver initial (optional)

WHAT YOU DO

1. Plan the design of the wreath by laying out all of the elements on a flat surface.

2. On a covered surface and in a well-ventilated area, spray-paint the pinecones and sticks with the chrome spray paint. Let dry.

3. Wire the pinecones into the wreath. Tuck or wire the sticks into the wreath.

4. Wind the tinsel through the wreath. Secure tinsel with wire if necessary.

5. Wire the ornaments and secure at the top inside of the wreath. Add a purchased metal initial if desired.

6. Make a large bow and secure at the top of the wreath with wire. Add a wire at the back for hanging.

COZY PLAID WREATH

Warm strips of plaid flannel wrap up a simple wreath form to make a cozy wreath to hang by the fireplace.

WHAT YOU NEED

Cotton flannel in desired patterns and colors • Scissors • 12-inch plastic foam round wreath form • Short straight pins • Pinking shears • Red jingle bells • Fresh greenery

WHAT YOU DO

1. Cut the flannel into 2-inch strips and wrap around the wreath form using different patterns and colors of fabric. Pin in place.
2. Using pinking shears, cut approximately 10 squares of flannel from different patterns and colors. Fold the squares in half and in half again to find the middle. Open up, and pin closely together on the wreath, creating a focal point. Pin the red jingle bells in the center of the tucked squares.
3. Cut a 3-inch-wide strip of flannel and loop around the top for hanging. Tuck pieces of greenery under the loop.

CIRCULAR MOTION

Select fresh herbs, evergreen sprigs, and leafy stems in varying hues, shapes, and textures to pile on the pizzazz.

WHAT YOU NEED

8-inch-diameter twig wreath form • Fresh Norfolk pine, blue spruce, cedar, and/or Scotch pine sprigs • Lemon leaves • Silica-dried red poinsettia leaves or artificial poinsettia leaves • Pepper berries • Pinecones • Hot-glue gun and glue sticks

WHAT YOU DO

1. Glue evergreen sprigs to the wreath form to create a lush foundation. Glue on (or tuck in) a ring of layered lemon leaves with all leaves facing the same direction.
2. Arrange and glue preserved poinsettia leaves amid the lemon leaves. Glue on berries and pinecones to fill out the wreath.

WHITE TIE-ON WREATH

Create a winter wonderland of white using strips of neutral white fabrics and a pretty bow.

WHAT YOU NEED
20-inch-diameter wire wreath form • 4 yards of white burlap • 3 yards of copper 3-inch-wide ribbon • 3 yards of sheer tan 2-inch-wide ribbon • Florists wire

WHAT YOU DO
1. Cut burlap into two-hundred-eighty 1×16-inch strips. Starting on inner ring of the wire wreath form, tie strips to the wire ring, adding the same number of strips to each ring segment.
2. Continue adding strips to each ring. Use six strips in each inner ring segment, seven strips in each second and third ring segment, and eight strips in each outer ring segment. For a fuller look, add more strips.
3. Fold each ribbon into a large loop bow. Wire the bows to the top of the wreath.

POM-POM PERFECTION

Keep the look crisp and light using pure white pom-poms to create this soft and sweet wreath.

WHAT YOU NEED
Large pom-pom maker (we used 3⅜-inch) (available at crafts stores) • Super bulky yarn: cream • Flat florists wreath form (in the diameter of your choice) • Fabric glue, such as Fabri-Tac, or hot-glue gun and glue sticks • ⅜-inch pom-pom trim • Decorative ribbon

WHAT YOU DO
1. Following the instructions on the pom-pom maker and using cream bulky yarn, make enough pom-poms to cover the front of the wreath form.
2. Glue pom-poms to wreath form using fabric glue or a hot-glue gun. Glue one end of the pom-pom trim to the back of the wreath form, wind the trim around the wreath, filling spaces between the larger pom-poms. Glue trim end to back of wreath. Add a decorative ribbon for a hanger.

BERRY BRIGHT

Classic Christmas colors and a pretty plaid bow make this faux-greenery wreath one you can use year after year.

WHAT YOU NEED

Artificial mixed pine sprays with attached pinecones and berries • Hot-glue gun and glue sticks • 12-inch-diameter grapevine wreath • Artificial angel pine sprays • Artificial red berry stems • 1¾ yards of 2½-inch-wide wire-edge ribbon • Florists wire

WHAT YOU DO

1. Trim the stems of four mixed pine sprays as necessary. Hot-glue the sprays on top of the grapevine wreath, spacing them evenly and letting the greenery fall in a clockwise direction (Photo 1, above).

2. Fill in bare spots by hot-gluing additional mixed pine sprays to the wreath, letting the greenery fall in a clockwise direction. Continue adding sprays until the wreath looks full (Photo 2).

3. Hot-glue the angel pine sprays to the wreath, angling sprays clockwise (Photo 3).

4. Hot-glue the berry sprays to the wreath, angling them clockwise (Photo 4).

5. Wire or hot-glue a bow to the wreath top (Photo 5). To make the bow, cut a 40-inch length of ribbon. Leaving a 10-inch tail, make a 5-inch loop, holding the ribbon between your thumb and index finger. Continuing to hold the ribbon, make a second loop the same size in the opposite direction. Make another equal-size loop in the same direction as the first loop. Wrap wire around the bow center; do not trim wire. For the remaining bow tails, twist the bow wire around the center of the remaining piece of ribbon. Trim the wire and ribbon tails.

BOUNTIFUL WINTER BEAUTY

Broken twigs picked up from the backyard or purchased at a crafts store are spray-painted white to unify this beautifully textured wreath.

WHAT YOU NEED

12-inch white or natural grapevine wreath with a flat face • White matte spray paint • Petite pinecones • Hot-glue gun and glue sticks • 4- to 8-inch sticks • ⅜-inch jute ribbon • Cedar sprigs

WHAT YOU DO

1. Paint a natural grapevine wreath white or start with a white wreath. Lightly spray-paint a few pinecones with a dusting of white. Let dry. Use a hot-glue gun to evenly adhere the longest sticks to the wreath; fill in with smaller pieces, gluing them if needed.

2. Lightly spray the entire wreath with white paint, letting some of the natural colors of the sticks show through. Glue on pinecones. Tie a jute ribbon bow near the top center of the wreath. Finish the wreath with cedar sprigs tucked behind the bow.

GREEN TINSEL-GARLAND WREATH

Yards of bright and shiny tinsel garland wrap around a foam wreath form to make a quick-as-a-wink wreath for a mantel or door.

WHAT YOU NEED

12-inch round plastic foam wreath • 4-yard length of wide green tinsel garland • Short straight pins

WHAT YOU DO

1. Starting at one end of the garland, pin in place on the foam wreath.

2. Wrap the garland around the wreath, being sure to cover the entire wreath form. Pin the end in place.

BRIGHT AND SHINY RED WREATH

Ornaments in classic Christmas red are lined up to make a dazzling wreath for the holidays.

WHAT YOU NEED

12-inch plastic foam round wreath form • 2 to 3 yards of 1-inch-wide ribbon in color to match ornaments • Short straight pins • Boxes of small red ball ornaments • Hot-glue gun and hot-glue sticks • Wide ribbon for hanging

WHAT YOU DO

1. Wrap the foam wreath form with the ribbon, securing the ends with short pins.

2. Remove the tops of the ornaments. Apply hot glue to the top of each ornament and press into the wreath form. Continue until all of the front and sides are covered with the ornaments.

3. Loop the wide ribbon around the top of the wreath.

MINI CANDY WREATH

Pint-size wreath forms are wrapped with ribbon and rickrack to create sweet candylike holiday decor.

WHAT YOU NEED

7-inch plastic foam wreath form • 1-inch-wide white satin ribbon • Scissors • Short straight pins • Jumbo red or apple green rickrack • Printed ribbon for hanging

WHAT YOU DO

1. Starting at one end, wrap the wreath form with the white satin ribbon, pinning in place. Continue until entire wreath is covered.

2. Starting on the back side, pin one end of the rickrack to the wrapped form. Wrap it around the form, leaving space between the rickrack. Pin in place. Loop a printed ribbon through the top for hanging.

Deck the halls with wreaths in all sizes and shapes. Use a variety of materials such as painted sticks, bright red ornaments, shiny green tinsel, and jumbo rickrack to create the perfect wreath for each corner of your holiday home.

Merry and Bright

A fresh and lively color scheme sets the tone
for a bright and happy Christmas.

BRIGHT FELT FLOWER ORNAMENTS

Bright colors in nonwoven felt are embroidered to make heirloom trims.

WHAT YOU NEED

Nonwoven felt such as National Nonwovens in bright colors • Scissors • Needle • Embroidery floss • Sequins • Seed beads • Fabric glue • Polyester fiberfill stuffing • Fine string for hanging

WHAT YOU DO

1. Enlarge and trace the pattern templates, right, and cut out. Choose the desired colors and cut two of the background color and one of the front color.

2. Using desired embroidery stitches, stitch designs on the front piece of felt, making crisscross designs. Sew sequins in the center of the design and on the piece as desired. Add a seed bead to the center of each sequin.

3. Adhere the stitched piece to one of the background pieces using fabric glue.

4. Place the layered piece atop the other background piece. Use the buttonhole stitch to secure around the edges, leaving a small space to stuff slightly with fiberfill. Stuff slightly. Finish stitching around the piece.

5. Add any other embellishments such as seed beads around the edge of the piece. Add a string for hanging.

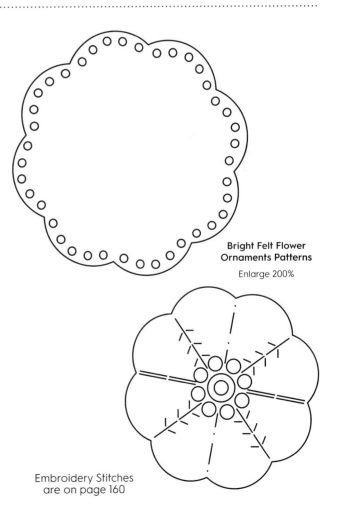

Bright Felt Flower Ornaments Patterns

Enlarge 200%

Embroidery Stitches are on page 160

BRIGHT POINSETTIA GARLAND

Use tried-and-true Christmas red to make the holiday bright and happy. Bright red paper poinsettias frame this cozy fireplace.

WHAT YOU NEED

Roll of 19½-inch-wide heavyweight red and green crepe paper • 24-gauge cloth-covered green florists wire • Crafts glue • Green florists tape • Artificial stamens • Hot-glue gun and glue sticks

WHAT YOU DO

DIRECTIONS FOR FLOWERS

1. Enlarge and trace the template patterns, right. Unroll crepe paper, noting direction of the ridges that run the length of the paper. Place a bract pattern on the crepe paper so a ridge runs through the center of the pattern; trace and cut out. Repeat with each pattern to cut 2 or 3 small bracts, 2 or 3 medium bracts, and 5 or 6 large bracts. If desired, cut 2 or 3 leaves from green crepe paper in the same manner.

2. From florists wire, cut a 5-inch length for each small bract, a 6-inch length for each medium bract, and a 7-inch length for each large bract and each leaf. Run a line of crafts glue along the ridge on the back of a bract and adhere appropriate wire on the glue line, placing the wire end approximately ¼ inch from the bract tip. Repeat for each bract and leaf. Let dry.

3. Gently fold each bract and leaf in half along the wire with wrong sides together. Gently pull on the edges of each piece to create a slightly ruffled effect. Twist bottom edges around wire stems.

4. To assemble the flower, gather the ends of small and medium bracts, then place large bracts behind the small and medium bracts; secure with florists tape. Add leaves behind the bracts and wrap tape around all wires. Add artificial stamens to the center of each flower and use hot glue to secure. **Note:** If flower becomes too top-heavy, add a length of wire to the wire bundle for support. Cover with tape.

DIRECTIONS FOR GARLAND

1. To construct the garland, cut the wire stems on each flower to a 5-inch length. Weave the flower stems into a piece of ⅜-inch cording at evenly spaced intervals. Tuck the ends of 12-inch lengths of ribbon between each flower. Finish with assorted greens, stabilizing with hot glue if necessary.

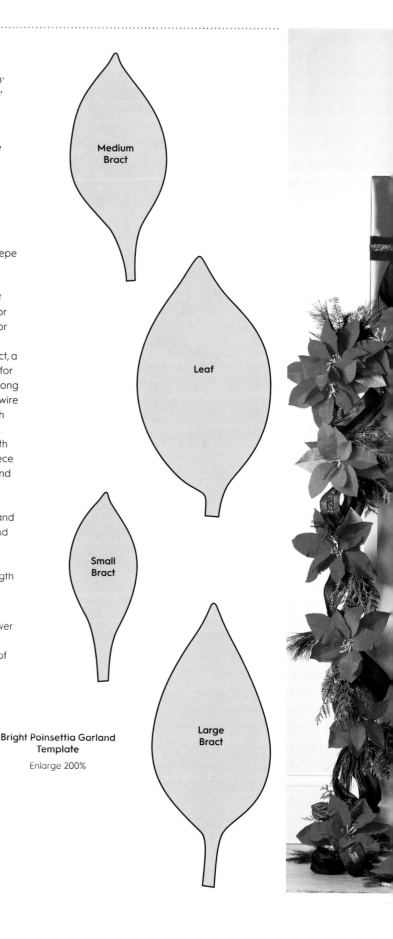

Medium Bract

Leaf

Small Bract

Large Bract

Bright Poinsettia Garland Template

Enlarge 200%

Packages wrapped in classic red papers and tied with same-hue ribbons and trims add a strong focal point on the mantel. Showcased with the poinsettia garland, the look is festive and bright.

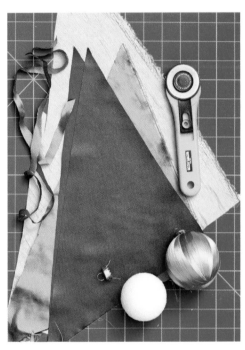

FABRIC-RIBBON ORNAMENTS

All colors of bright and shiny fabrics are cut on the bias and wrapped around foam balls, creating elegant trims for your holiday tree.

WHAT YOU NEED

Foam balls such as Styrofoam balls about 2½ inches in diameter • Silk or polyester fabric • Rotary cutter • Long ruler • Cutting mat • Silk or polyester fabric, about ½ yard of each type of fabric. • Hot-glue gun and glue sticks • Metallic hanging toppers from old ornaments • Short sewing pins • Elastic ribbon (optional)

WHAT YOU DO

1. Using the rotary cutter, ruler, and the mat, cut fabric on the bias into strips ½- to ¾-inch wide. Cut about 10 strips per ornament, each about 16 inches long.

Note: If you are making many ornaments, purchase more fabric so strips can be longer.

2. Attach the strips of fabric around the foam ball using a dab of hot glue at the top of the ornament. Keep wrapping the strips around the ornament, overlapping slightly each time, adding strips as needed. When the ornament is covered, secure with hot glue.

3. When dry, push one sewing pin through the top of the ornament. Attach a top from an old ornament with hot glue pushing into the ball.

Note: Elastic ribbon can also be used to wrap the balls. Wrap the ball and follow Steps 2 and 3 for finishing.

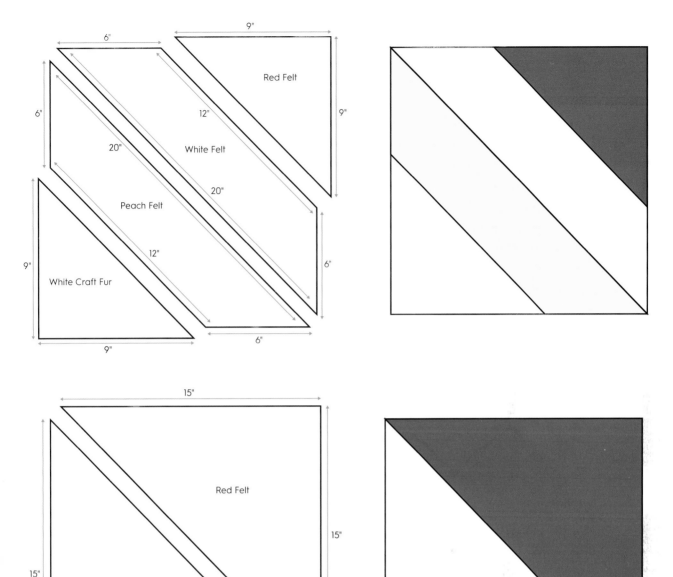

HAPPY SANTA PILLOW

This geometric fellow will bring a smile to any corner of your house. Made from simple shapes, he can be made in the blink of an eye.

WHAT YOU NEED

Nonwoven felt such as National Nonwovens in cream, red, and white. • Scissors • Two black buttons • White craft fur • Large pom-pom • Sewing machine • Polyester fiberfill or pillow stuffing • Black thread • White thread • Needle • Hot-glue gun and glue sticks

WHAT YOU DO

1. Using the cutting diagram, above, cut out all pattern pieces. Sew front pieces together and then back pieces together using a ¼-inch seam. Before attaching the front to the back of the pillow, sew on the button eyes with needle and thread. Attach the mustache with hot glue.

2. With right sides facing, sew the pillow front to the pillow back, allowing room to turn the pillow inside out. When done, turn the pillow inside out, stuff with polyester fiberfill, and hand-sew shut.

3. Attach pom-pom on the top of hat with needle and thread.

COZY SWEATER PILLOW

*Repurpose a castaway sweater into a bright holiday
accent pillow for your favorite cozy couch.*

WHAT YOU NEED

Castaway sweater with cable stitching • Scissors • Iron •
Sewing machine • Polyester fiberfill • Thread to match color
of pillow • Large silver button or pin • Needle

WHAT YOU DO

1. Lay out the sweater and plan the size and design of the
pillow. Cut two rectangular-shape pieces from the sweater for
the front and back of the pillow. Press the pieces.
2. Cut off the ends of the sleeves. Set aside.
3. With right sides together, stitch the front and back together,
leaving an opening for turning. Turn; stuff with fiberfill and sew
opening closed.
4. Form the rosette using one or both of the sleeve ends. Use
a running stitch to gather up the edge of the cut piece. Pull
up and use needle and thread to secure. Turn under. Sew the
button or pin to the middle. Sew to the corner of the pillow.

EASY HOLIDAY TOTE BAG

*Dress up a purchased tote bag for the holidays with a
simple running stitch and some oversize buttons.*

WHAT YOU NEED

Purchased canvas or burlap bag (available at crafts stores)
• Buttons • String such as bakers twine • Large needle to
accommodate twine • Hot-glue gun and glue sticks

WHAT YOU DO

1. Plan the design based on the size and shape of the bag.
Using a running stitch and bakers twine, stitch down the bag
vertically. At the end of the row, sew on a button using the
bakers twine.

2. Tie bows with the twine and attach with hot glue.

FELT GLASS SLIPS

Bright colors of felt and a few stitches will dress up ho-hum drinking glasses for festive party fun.

WHAT YOU NEED

Felt in desired color • Water-soluble marking pen • 13-inch length of contrasting pom-pom trim • Fabric glue • Embroidery floss in color to match pom-pom trim

WHAT YOU DO

1. Trace circle pattern, below, including dashed lines and center square, onto white paper; cut out the circle. Cut along the dashed lines and cut out center square.

2. Using the outside edge of pattern, cut 2 circles from felt. Set aside 1 felt circle for coaster bottom. Using a water-soluble marking pen, trace the center square onto the remaining felt circle and draw through pattern's cut lines. Cut along the drawn lines and cut out center square from the felt circle to create the coaster top.

3. Use fabric glue to adhere pom-pom trim to the outside edge of coaster bottom, overlapping trim ends; let dry.

4. Using 6 strands of embroidery floss, stitch French knots, running stitches, cross-stitches, or straight stitches about ¼ inch inside the outside edge of coaster top.

5. With the wrong side up, run a thin line of fabric glue around the edge of coaster bottom. Place coaster top wrong side down on top of coaster bottom; let dry.

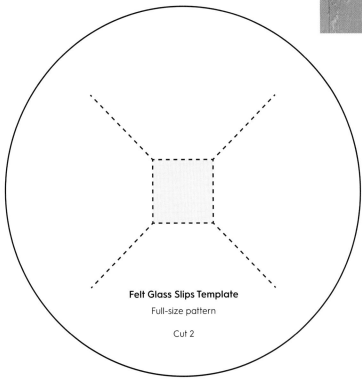

Felt Glass Slips Template

Full-size pattern

Cut 2

STRIPED PICTURE FRAME
Drinking straws in bright holiday colors line up to make a
clever frame to showcase your sweet little one.

WHAT YOU NEED
Purchased picture frame with wide mat • Drinking straws
in desired colors • Scissors • Ruler • Pencil • Hot-glue gun
and glue sticks • Mat cutter (optional) • Small pieces of
cardboard for spacers (optional)

WHAT YOU DO
1. Remove the mat from the frame. Plan the design based on
the frame and mat size.
2. Lay out the straws on the mat diagonally and mark where to
cut each one using a ruler. Cut the straws diagonally.
3. Use hot glue to glue the straws in place. Trim edges if
necessary using a mat cutter.
4. Place spacers around the edge of the mat if necessary and
place mat back into the frame.

SNOW TWOSOME

What's better than one snowman? A pair! The ivory felt snowman and snowwoman are sewn using the same pattern, but the differences are in the details.

WHAT YOU NEED

FOR EACH SNOW PERSON:

6×9-inch piece of ivory felt • Scrap of coral felt • Disappearing-ink marking pen • Black and ivory embroidery floss • Embroidery and sewing needles • Embroidery scissors or awl • 2 black 8-millimeter shank-back safety eyes • Wire cutters • Pink color pencil • Black and coral sewing thread • Polyester fiberfill • Flat toothpick • Crafts glue • Paintbrush

FOR THE SNOWMAN:

Felt scraps: black, olive green, mint green, white • 3 red seed beads • 4-inch chenille stems: 1 red and 1 white • Glitter: black, dark pink, silver

FOR THE SNOWWOMAN:

Felt scrap: ivory (collar) and lavender (buttons) • Glitter: pink, red, aqua • Metallic-green chenille stem • 6 inches of 28-gauge wire • Jewelry pliers • 2 pink 1-inch-diameter pom-poms • Pink sewing thread

WHAT YOU DO

CUT FABRICS

1. Trace patterns, page 85, onto white paper; cut out. Trace each shape onto appropriate colors of felt using disappearing-ink marking pen; cut out. Use one strand of floss for all embroidery.

ASSEMBLE HEAD AND BODY FOR EITHER SNOWPERSON

1. Using black floss, stitch the mouth and eyebrows with running stitches. Carefully poke a tiny hole for each eye. Insert the eye shank through each hole. Slide the washer onto the shank. Trim each shank, leaving about ⅛ inch.

2. Using black, straight-stitch eyelashes on snowwoman. Color the cheeks with pink color pencil.

3. Whipstitch darts at tops of front and back head pieces, stitching them on the wrong side of felt.

4. Pin together head front and back pieces with wrong sides together. Using ivory floss, blanket-stitch around the head, leaving an opening at the bottom. Stuff head firmly with polyester fiberfill; stitch opening closed. Leave a long floss tail to attach head to body.

ADD THE DETAILS

1. Fold nose lengthwise in half. Beginning at the narrow end, blanket-stitch edges together using coral sewing thread. Using a flat toothpick, push tiny bits of fiberfill into the nose. Whipstitch the nose to the head.

2. Brush crafts glue onto the snowman's buttons. Sprinkle black glitter onto the glue; let dry. Stitch black buttons to snowman front or lavender buttons to snowwoman front.

3. Using ivory floss, whipstitch darts at tops and bottoms of front and back body pieces, sewing them on wrong side of felt. Pin together body front and back pieces with wrong

sides together. Use ivory floss to blanket-stitch around body, leaving neck open. Stuff body firmly with fiberfill.

4. Sew a gathering stitch around neck; pull threads to close the neck. Whipstitch opening closed.

5. With right sides together and using ivory floss, stitch arms together in pairs, leaving an opening on convex side of each arm. Firmly stuff arms with polyester fiberfill and whipstitch openings closed.

6. Pin head to neck; whipstitch together.

FINISH THE SNOWMAN

1. Pin arms to sides of body. With 2 strands of ivory floss, insert the needle under one arm and push it through the body and out through the other arm. Stitch back and forth a few times to secure the arms.

2. Brush crafts glue onto the hatband. Sprinkle dark pink glitter onto the glue; let dry. Align one long edge of hatband with a long edge of hat side; stitch in place. Using black floss, blanket-stitch together short edges of hat side to form a cylinder. Blanket-stitch hat crown to top of cylinder. Gently stuff hat with fiberfill. Blanket-stitch hat to hat brim. Whipstitch the bottom of hat to head.

3. Thread needle with ivory floss; stitch 3 red seed beads to holly leaves. Stitch holly to side of hat brim.

4. Stitch scarf neckband at back of neck. Do not cut or tie off thread. Snip fringe on each end of scarf tie. Fold scarf tie so one tail is ½ inch longer than the other. Slide scarf tie over scarf neckband, positioning it slightly off-center at front of snowman; pin. Wrap neckband around neck until neckband ends meet. Use thread tail to stitch ends together. Push needle through seam at base of head and out through the center of folded scarf tie in front. Take a tiny stitch, then push needle back through the folded scarf piece and through the seam at base of head. Repeat a few times to anchor scarf.

5. Referring to photo, twist together red and white chenille stems, bending an end to form a candy cane.

6. Brush crafts glue onto white felt bow. Sprinkle silver glitter onto wet glue; let dry. Shake off excess. Blanket-stitch together the two short edges of bow. Wrap bow center around bow; stitch bow center edges to back of bow. Stitch bow to candy cane and stitch candy cane to a snowman arm.

FINISH THE SNOWWOMAN

1. Referring to photo, pin arms to sides of body; attach arms as for the snowman. Brush glue onto collar. Sprinkle pink glitter onto wet glue; let dry. Shake off excess.

2. With ivory floss, stitch collar to the body.

3. Fold green chenille stem in half. Twist the halves together, forming a thicker stem. Shape stem into a circle and twist together ends to form a wreath. Brush glue onto bow. Sprinkle red glitter onto wet glue; let dry. Shake off excess. Stitch bow to bottom of wreath. Stitch wreath to snowwoman's hands.

4. Brush crafts glue onto 28-gauge wire. Sprinkle aqua glitter onto wet glue; let dry. Bend glittered wire into a U shape that will fit snugly on head. Use jewelry pliers to curl a tiny loop at each end of wire.

5. Position wire on head, placing each looped end on the seam at the ear area. Stitch a pom-pom over each wire end.

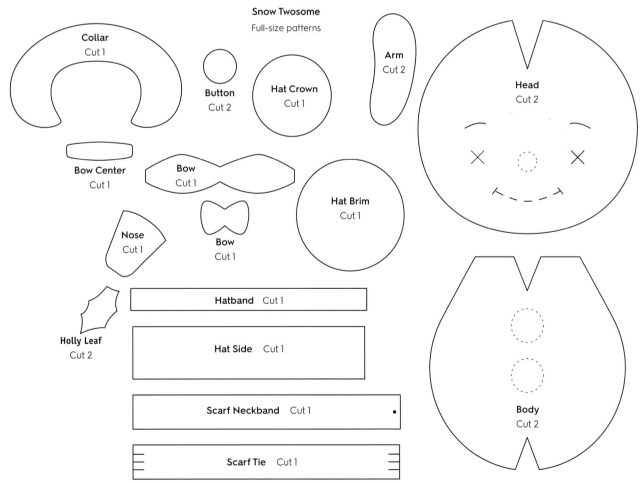

Snow Twosome

Full-size patterns

Collar Cut 1

Button Cut 2

Hat Crown Cut 1

Arm Cut 2

Head Cut 2

Bow Center Cut 1

Bow Cut 1

Hat Brim Cut 1

Nose Cut 1

Bow Cut 1

Holly Leaf Cut 2

Hatband Cut 1

Hat Side Cut 1

Scarf Neckband Cut 1

Scarf Tie Cut 1

Body Cut 2

Wrap It Up

Whether you wrap your packages tied up with strings or with a sparkling bow, make your gift wrap just as personal as the gift inside.

BROWN PAPER PACKAGES TIED UP IN STRINGS

Keep your packages beautifully simple with brown paper and all kinds of unexpected embellishments.

DOILY TIE-UP

WHAT YOU NEED

Wrapped brown-paper box • Natural color or brown paper doilies • Scissors • Crafts glue • Brown and white bakers twine • Red and cream buttons • Alphabet sticker • Brown gift tag

WHAT YOU DO

1. Plan the arrangement on the box. Lay the doilies on the box and glue in place. Tuck and lay one doily on top of the other and glue only in the center.
2. Stack and thread bakers twine in the holes of the buttons. Glue buttons in place.
3. Adhere the alphabet sticker to the gift tag. Tie bakers twine around the box and tie a bow. Add the gift tag.

PAINT PRINT BOXES

WHAT YOU NEED

Brown kraft paper • Masking tape • Box to wrap • Clear wrapping tape • Scissors • Double-stick tape • White and lime green acrylic paint • Small piece of cardboard • Jingle bells, pinecones, and small ornaments • Bakers twine • Fresh evergreen sprig

WHAT YOU DO

1. Lay the kraft paper on a flat surface and tape down edges with masking tape.
2. Randomly place small pools of paint on the paper. Use the small piece of cardboard to pull the paint across the paper, creating a random design. Let dry.
3. Wrap the box with the paper. Tie the string around the box, tying on the jingle bells, ornaments, and pinecones and using double-stick tape to secure if necessary. Tuck in greenery where desired.

STAMPED BERRY BOX

WHAT YOU NEED

Brown kraft paper • Masking tape • Box to wrap • Clear wrapping tape • Scissors • Double-stick tape • Red and lime green acrylic paint • Round sponge foam brushes • Rubber bands • Pencil with eraser • Flat red ribbon • String • Candy cane • Artificial red berries • Fresh evergreen sprig

WHAT YOU DO

1. Lay the kraft paper on a flat surface and tape down edges with masking tape.
2. Use the round sponge brush to make large red dots to look like berries. Dip the end of the pencil eraser in red paint to make small berries. Use scissors to cut another foam brush into a leaf shape. Use green paint to make leaves. Cut the rubber bands and dip into green paint to make the stems (See Photo A). Let dry.
3. Wrap gift box with the printed paper. Use double-stick tape to secure the ribbon on the box. Wrap the string around the ribbon. Tuck in the candy cane, berries, and evergreen and secure with double-stick tape.

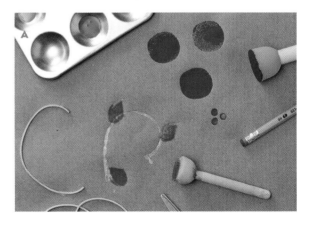

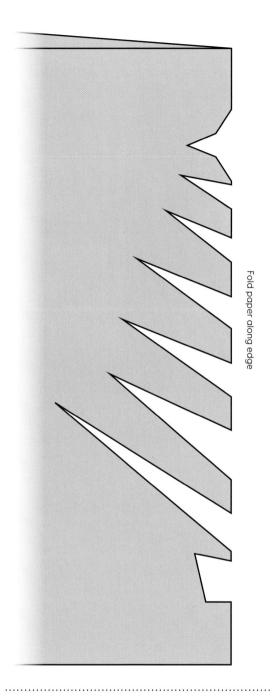

Cut-Out Tree Wraps
Patterns

Fold paper along edge

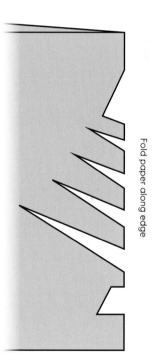

Fold paper along edge

CUT-OUT TREE WRAPS

WHAT YOU NEED

Brown kraft paper • Pencil • Scissors • Iron • Box to wrap • Clear wrapping tape • Double-stick tape • Fabric in desired print or style • Bakers twine and other string or trims • Crafts glue

WHAT YOU DO

1. Trace the template patterns, above. Cut wrapping paper long enough to wrap the gift. Fold the paper in half and mark the cut areas with a pencil. Cut out the desired design. Lay the paper on an ironing board and use low setting of iron to smooth paper.

2. Wrap the box with desired fabric first using double-stick tape to secure. Then wrap the box with the cut design, securing with tape or glue.

3. Trim the box with twine and other trims, gluing or taping in place.

ALL THAT GLITTERS ... SILVER AND GOLD

Make your gifts sparkle with silver and gold paint and holiday trims.

BEADED SNOWFLAKE BAUBLE

A bright metallic paper set off with winter white paper and a hand-beaded trim says you really care. Use like-color beads or go for colorful metallic beads.

WHAT YOU NEED
White wrapping paper • Gold wrapping paper • White acrylic crafts paint • Toothbrush • 1½-inch-wide moss green satin ribbon • 4½-inch wire snowflake form • Small round wooden and imitation bone beads • Quick-setting gel glue • Adhesive dots

WHAT YOU DO
1. Wrap gift in white paper.
2. To make snow-dusted gold paper, set gold paper faceup on a flat surface. Dip a toothbrush into white paint diluted with water; run a finger across the bristles to spatter paint on paper. Let dry.
3. Wrap the gold paper around the package, leaving a few inches of white paper showing at the top. Tie a moss green ribbon around the package where the two papers meet. Finish with a bow.
4. To make a snowflake topper, string beads onto the wire snowflake form, working on one wire at a time. Apply glue to each wire end, push on the final bead, and hold it in place until the glue sets. Attach the snowflake to the bow using an adhesive dot.

ALL THAT GLITTERS

An hourglass shape formed from glitter paper triangles edged with green and gold washi tape proves that all that glitters is truly gift-wrapping gold.

WHAT YOU NEED
White wrapping paper • Scrap paper • Glitter wrapping paper • Double-stick tape • Green washi tape • Metallic gold washi tape • ½-inch-wide gold-edged green satin ribbon • Pinecone pick

WHAT YOU DO
1. Wrap the package in white paper.
2. To make glitter paper triangles, cut a piece of scrap paper to the same size as the face of your package. Fold it diagonally from corner to corner in two directions to create an X in the center.
3. Cut out the top triangle to use as a template for cutting 2 triangles from the glitter wrapping paper. Tape the glitter paper triangles to the front of the package using double-stick tape.
4. Apply green washi tape along outer edges of triangles to reinforce the X-shape. Top the green tape with narrow strips of gold washi tape.
5. Tie ribbon around package and insert pinecone pick into the bow.

CRISS-CROSS PACKAGE

Silver and gold paint stamped onto a white box make a clean and bright wrap for that special gift.

WHAT YOU NEED

White paper and box to wrap or white box • Scrap piece of wood • Yarn • Craft paint in silver and gold • Paper plate • Foam brush • Ribbon • Double-stick tape • Small sticks • Gold bird or pinecones

WHAT YOU DO

1. Plan the design on the paper or box. Wrap yarn around scrap piece of wood in an organic or geometric pattern depending on the look you want to achieve.

2. Put paint on a paper plate and brush out to an even thickness on the plate. Dip the stamp into the paint and stamp onto paper or onto gift box repeatedly (See Photo A). Let dry.

3. Wrap the box if using paper. Secure the ribbons around the box. Tie on pinecones or tuck in the sticks and tie on the bird.

A

WOODLAND STAR

Cut a galaxy's worth of stellar shapes using thin sheets of wood and green felt. Add ribbons in varying shades of green to underscore the natural yet glittering look.

WHAT YOU NEED

White wrapping paper • White wrapping paper with embossed pattern • Double-stick tape • ⅝-inch-wide ivory/gold metallic ribbon • ½-inch-wide olive green satin ribbon • Wood veneer sheet with paper backing • Scissors or crafts knife • Green felt • Quick-setting gel glue • Glittered floral spray or pick

WHAT YOU DO

1. Wrap the gift in white paper.

2. Center a panel of embossed paper on the package, taping to the back of the gift. Layer ivory/gold and olive green ribbon strips; wrap and tape ends of perpendicular pieces to back. Tape or glue a loosely tied ivory/gold ribbon bow on top of the ribbons.

3. To make the star, copy and enlarge template, below. Cut out. Trace the template onto the back of the wood sheet and cut out. Set star on top of the felt. Glue in place and trim excess felt.

4. Glue small pieces of glittered floral stems at the top of the star. Tuck the star beneath the bow and tape in place.

Woodland Star Pattern
Enlarge 200%

MISTLETOE TRIM

Cardstock is topped with green leaf cutouts and beaded details, then adhered to the gift for a stunning wrap.

WHAT YOU NEED

White wrapping paper • Ivory crafts paper • Leaf stamp • Green ink pad • White cardstock • Quick-setting gel glue • Miniature wood beads • Gold foil washi tape • ½-inch-wide gold-edged brown ribbon

WHAT YOU DO

1. Wrap the package in white paper.

2. Stamp leaf shapes onto ivory paper; let dry. Cut out leaf shapes and lightly crease their centers. Arrange the leaves on a piece of cardstock cut to fit the front of the package; apply a line of glue along the crease on the back of each leaf and glue leaves to cardstock.

3. Glue clusters of beads at bases of leaves. Attach the leafed cardstock to the package with strips of gold washi tape.

4. Wrap ribbon around the package, tying it so the knot falls between the leafy sprigs.

SPARKLING STRAWS STAR WRAP

Cut drinking straws make shiny stars to attach to any holiday wrap.

WHAT YOU NEED

Striped metallic paper straws • Hot-glue gun and glue sticks • Package wrapped in metallic print or plain paper • Green ribbon • Alphabet letter in metallic gold or painted gold • Desired color of string

WHAT YOU DO

1. To make the straw stars, cut straws in half or to desired length at a 45-degree angle. Secure straws together with hot glue. Set aside.

2. Trim package with ribbon or string. Hot-glue stars on top of package. Add alphabet letter.

Embellishments made from crafts paper and paper drinking straws combine with pretty ribbons to dress up gift giving this holiday season.

COLOR IT CHRISTMAS

Use paint, crayons, colored pencils, or bright velvet ribbons to give your packages a personal touch.

BUBBLE WRAP DOTTED WRAP

WHAT YOU NEED
Matte-finish white wrapping paper • Scissors • Strip of bubble wrap • Small foam roller • Red acrylic craft paint • Black striped ribbon • Holly berry pick • Gift tag • Merry Christmas stamp and stamp pad

WHAT YOU DO
1. Cut a piece of white wrapping paper to the desired size. If needed, weight down the edges to keep the paper flat. Place bubble wrap bubble side up on a flat surface. Roll a thin, even layer of red acrylic craft paint across the bubble wrap. Turn bubble wrap over and press it onto the wrapping paper; smooth bubble wrap with your hands to ensure even printing.
2. Remove bubble wrap and let wrapping paper dry before handling. Wrap gift with the paper.
3. Embellish the package with black ribbon tied into a bow and a holly berry pick. Stamp "Merry Christmas" on a tag. Attach the tag to the bow.

PAPER TAPE PATTERNS WRAP

WHAT YOU NEED
Kraft paper • Washi tape: red with white trees, red with white dots, and black

WHAT YOU DO
1. Wrap a gift in kraft paper. Adhere strips of tree-pattern tape around the top edges and top side edges of the package. Adhere strips of dotted tape around the bottom side edges of the package. Adhere strips of black tape below and above the printed tapes on the sides.

TISSUE-PAPER FLOWERS WRAP

WHAT YOU NEED
Matte-finish white wrapping paper • Pencil • Scissors • Red tissue paper • Spray adhesive or glue stick

WHAT YOU DO
1. Wrap a gift in white paper. Trace the flower pattern, below, onto cardstock and cut out for a template.
2. Cut tissue paper into 3-inch squares. Following folding instructions, below, fold the squares as shown. Place the template on top of the folded paper, aligning template with folded edges, as shown in Step 4, below, and cut out.
3. Unfold the paper to reveal a flower shape. Adhere the tissue flowers around the gift's side edges using spray adhesive or a glue stick.

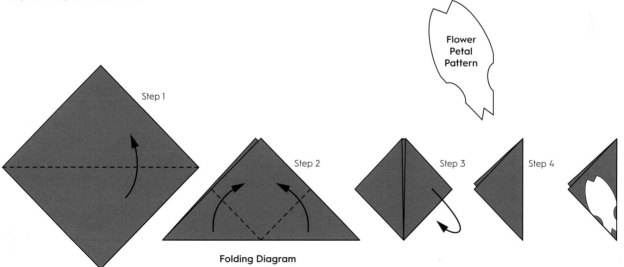

Flower Petal Pattern

Step 1

Step 2

Step 3

Step 4

Folding Diagram

COLORING BOOK WRAP

Copy those amazing colored-in papers and use them for a special gift wrap.

WHAT YOU NEED
Coloring book-style colored-in pages • Copy machine or scanner • Box to wrap • String or ribbon

WHAT YOU DO
1. Copy the colored pages or use the original to wrap the gift.
2. Trim package with ribbon or string. Add a gift tag if desired.

VELVET RIBBON WRAPS

Crayon-color velvet ribbons make colorful statements when wrapped around plain white boxes or packages. Stack the boxes and tie with bows or accordion-pleat the ribbon and add strings of beads and sequins.

Pretty and Pastel

Nontraditional colors of Christmas reflect the warmth of the season with pastel-colored projects that are winter-soft and sweet.

Pastel-swirled votives reflect the season with glitters of light while plain white bottle brush trees are spruced up with a touch of color and dozens of little pom-poms dyed to match.

DELICATE MARBELIZED VOTIVES

Pastel nail polish finds a new use when it is painted onto a clear votive holder for a simply elegant candle.

WHAT YOU NEED
Disposable container such as an old butter or yogurt container • Warm water • Nail polish • Toothpick • Glass votive • Fingernail polish remover (optional) • Crafts glue • Fine glitter • Votive candle

WHAT YOU DO
1. Be sure the glass votive is clean and dry.
2. Note: Always work in a well-ventilated area. Fill the disposable container with warm water. Drop a few drops of nail polish in and stir gently with toothpick. Working quickly, dip glass votive into water, rolling it along the top of the water.
3. Repeat until desired look is achieved. Use nail polish remover to remove any unwanted polish. Let dry completely. Run a fine line of crafts glue along the top of the votive. Dust top with glitter. Let dry. Add votive candle.

Never leave a burning candle unattended.

PASTEL BOTTLE BRUSH TREES

Plain white bottle brush trees are spruced up with pastel hues to create a pretty little forest.

WHAT YOU NEED
Disposable container deep enough to cover height of trees • White/natural bottle brush trees (available at crafts stores or online) • Fabric dye such as Rit in pastel colors • Mini pom-poms • Hair dryer (optional) • Crafts glue

WHAT YOU DO
1. Fill disposable container with hot water. Add dye to achieve desired color.
2. Dip the trees into the dye. Let the trees air dry. **TIP:** Once the trees are almost dry, use a hair dryer to dry them completely. It will get out all the excess water and fluff the branches.
3. To dye the pom-poms, let the pom-poms sit in the dye for 5 minutes, then remove. Lay out on a paper towel to dry completely.
4. Glue the pom-poms to the trees using little dots of crafts glue. Let dry.

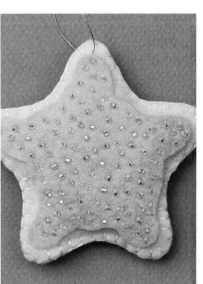

SUGAR COOKIE ORNAMENTS

Puffed-up sugar cookie trims will fool the eye and make everyone smile. Make a batch for yourself and one to give as a special gift.

WHAT YOU NEED

Nonwoven felt such as National Nonwovens in sugar cookie colors • Seed and small beads • Needle small enough to accommodate beads • Thin thread for hanging • Scissors • Pinking shears • Embroidery floss to match fabrics • Polyester fiberfill • Fine metallic string for hanging • Fabric glue

WHAT YOU DO

1. Trace the pattern templates, page 106, and cut out. Choose the desired colors and cut 2 of each pattern for the Candy Cane using pinking shears. Cut 2 for the Gingerbread Boy using regular scissors. For the Frosted Shapes, cut 2 of each cookie pattern and one of each frosting shape pattern.

2. For the candy cane, with wrong sides together, use embroidery floss and the running stitch to secure around the edges, leaving a small space to stuff slightly with polyester fiberfill. Stuff slightly. Finish stitching around the piece. Cut strips of red or pink felt and use fabric glue to glue the strips to the front of the candy cane.

3. For the Gingerbread Boy, sew beads to make a face and designs on the front piece.

4. For the Frosted Cookies, sew seed beads on the frosting-shape pieces to resembles sprinkles.

5. For all of the shapes except the candy cane, place the fronts and backs together with wrong sides facing. Use embroidery floss and the buttonhole stitch to secure around the edges, leaving a small space to stuff slightly with fiberfill. Stuff slightly. Finish stitching around the piece. Glue the frosting piece atop the cookie shapes for the Frosted Shapes.

6. Add a string for hanging all pieces.

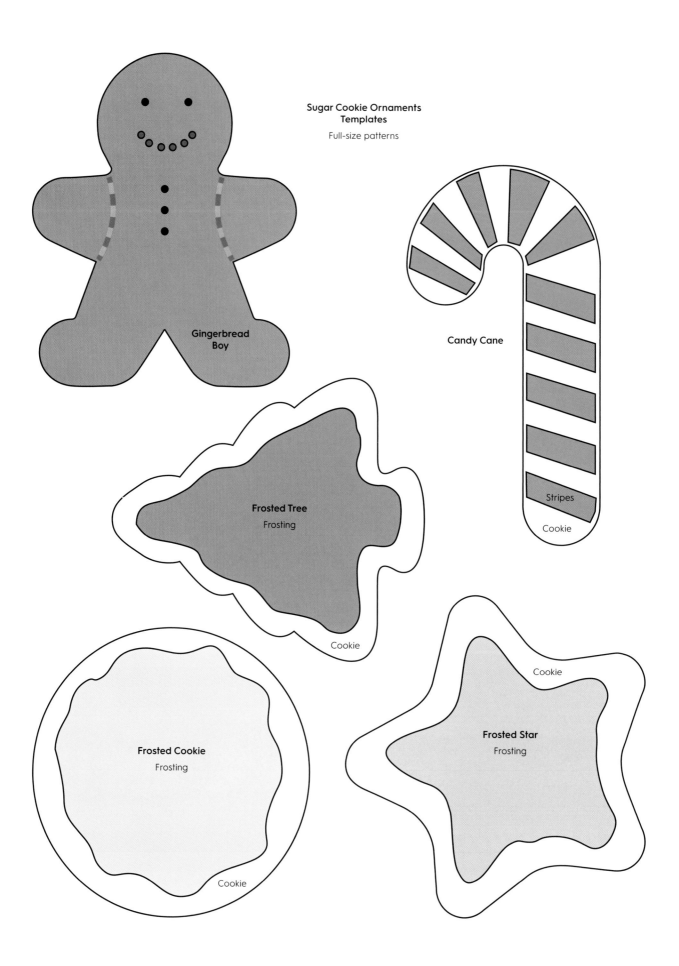

Sugar Cookie Ornaments
Templates

Full-size patterns

Gingerbread
Boy

Candy Cane

Stripes

Cookie

Frosted Tree

Frosting

Cookie

Frosted Cookie

Frosting

Cookie

Frosted Star

Frosting

Cookie

FLYING GEESE GARLAND

*Little squares of pastel felt are folded and tacked in place
to create a modern garland for your holiday tree.*

WHAT YOU NEED
Nonwoven felt such as National Nonwovens in pastel hues
• Scissors • Bakers twine/thick thread • Needle • Hot-glue
gun and glue sticks

WHAT YOU DO
1. Cut felt pieces into 2-inch squares, planning the design of
the garland.
2. Using a needle and bakers twine, sew through the center of
each square. Fold each square in half, aligning the points on
the string, and use a small dot of glue to adhere the felt piece
to the string. Repeat for entire garland.
3. Tie the ends of the twine.

Blank greeting cards from a crafts store can be transformed into handmade greeting cards with fun-to-use stickers and pretty scrapbook papers.

QUICK-AND-EASY GREETING CARDS

Holiday stickers and purchased greeting card blanks make quick work of making holiday cards.

WHAT YOU NEED

FOR THE TREE CARD:
Blank greeting cards in pastel colors • Pencil • Pastel snowflake stickers

FOR THE PHOTO CARD:
Blank photo greeting card in pastel colors • Scrapbook paper print with shapes large enough to cut out • Scissors • Crafts glue • Washi tape with holiday words

FOR THE PET CARD:
Blank greeting cards in pastel colors • Purchased pet or animal stickers and alphabet stickers • Pencil • Scrapbook paper print • Scissors • Crafts glue

WHAT YOU DO

FOR THE TREE CARD:
1. Plan the design of the card based on the size of the stickers by making a shape using dots with a pencil on the front of the card.
2. Adhere the stickers on the card, forming the shape.

FOR THE PHOTO CARD:
1. Plan the design of the card. Cut a piece of the scrapbook paper to fit the photo space. Glue inside the opening.
2. Cut another shape from the card and glue to the front.
3. Add a message using washi tape that has a message on it at the bottom.

FOR THE PET CARD:
1. Plan the design of the card based on the size of the stickers by marking where the stickers and letters will be placed.
2. Place the stickers on the front of the card.
3. Glue a piece of contrasting scrapbook paper to the back of the card.

SWEET CANDY WREATH TRIMS
Favorite Christmas candies are melted together to make the sweetest of holiday trims.

WHAT YOU NEED
Baking sheet • Aluminum foil • Pastel Christmas candies • Oven • Ribbon for hanging

WHAT YOU DO
1. Line a baking sheet with aluminum foil. Lay out the candies in a circle so they are just touching.
2. Put the candies in the cold oven. Preheat the oven to 250°F. Watching the candies carefully, melt the candies for about 5 minutes or until the candies have just melted. Ovens vary, so watch carefully. Remove the candies and let cool completely.
3. Loop a ribbon around the top for hanging.

GOLDEN PASTEL ORNAMENTS
Gold foil combines with soft hues of paint to make stunning trims for your holiday tree.

WHAT YOU NEED
Clear glass ornaments with removable tops • Acrylic paint in pastel colors • Water • Small bowl • Cotton balls • Foam brushes • Gold foil kit (gold foil sheets, adhesive, and sealer) • Ribbon for hanging

WHAT YOU DO
1. To color the ornaments, using a 10:1 ratio, mix acrylic paint and water in a bowl. Pour a small amount inside the clear ornament. Twist ornament around until the entire inside is covered. Put ornament upside down to dry.
2. When dry, apply gold foil adhesive with a foam brush to the top of the ornament following manufacturer's instructions. Press gold sheets onto the top of the ornament, using the cotton ball to press it into place, creating your pattern of choice, again following manufacturer's instructions. Let dry.
3. Apply gold foil sealer using a foam brush. Let dry. Add a ribbon for hanging.

SMITTEN FOR MITTENS

The beauty of these sweet little mittens is that you can whip one up in mere minutes. Tuck in a few candies and give as a gift.

WHAT YOU NEED

Freezer paper • 10×7-inch piece of ivory felt • Ivory sewing thread • Scallop-edge scissors or pinking shears • Fusible web • Desired embellishments: fabric scraps, scrap of green felt, 1-inch-diameter assorted felted balls, assorted iridescent and gold sequins, assorted ribbon

WHAT YOU DO

1. Trace pattern, page 113. Lay freezer paper, shiny side down, over mitten pattern; trace using a pencil. Cut out freezer-paper template outside drawn lines.

2. Fold felt in half to measure 5×7 inches. Using a hot dry iron, press freezer-paper template, shiny side down, onto ivory felt; let cool.

3. Using ivory thread, sew on the drawn template lines, leaving the cuff end open and stopping stitches where indicated by dots on mitten pattern. Carefully peel off freezer-paper template and cut out mitten approximately ⅛-inch outside stitched line.

4. Trim open edge of mitten with scallop-edge scissors; do not cut into stitches. Fold down edge for a cuff.

5. Embellish mitten as desired. To make holly, trace Holly Leaf pattern, page 113, and trace twice onto paper side of fusible web. Cut out around shapes. Using a hot dry iron, press fusible web, fusible side down, onto back of fabric scraps; cut out shapes on drawn lines. Peel off paper backings. Press fabric holly leaves onto green felt. Carefully cut around the fabric holly leaves, leaving a scant ⅛-inch felt border. Hand-stitch three felted balls in a cluster to the mitten cuff. Tuck holly leaf ends under the balls; stitch in place.

6. If desired, add a ribbon bow or hand-stitch sequins or small fabric squares to the mitten cuff or front.

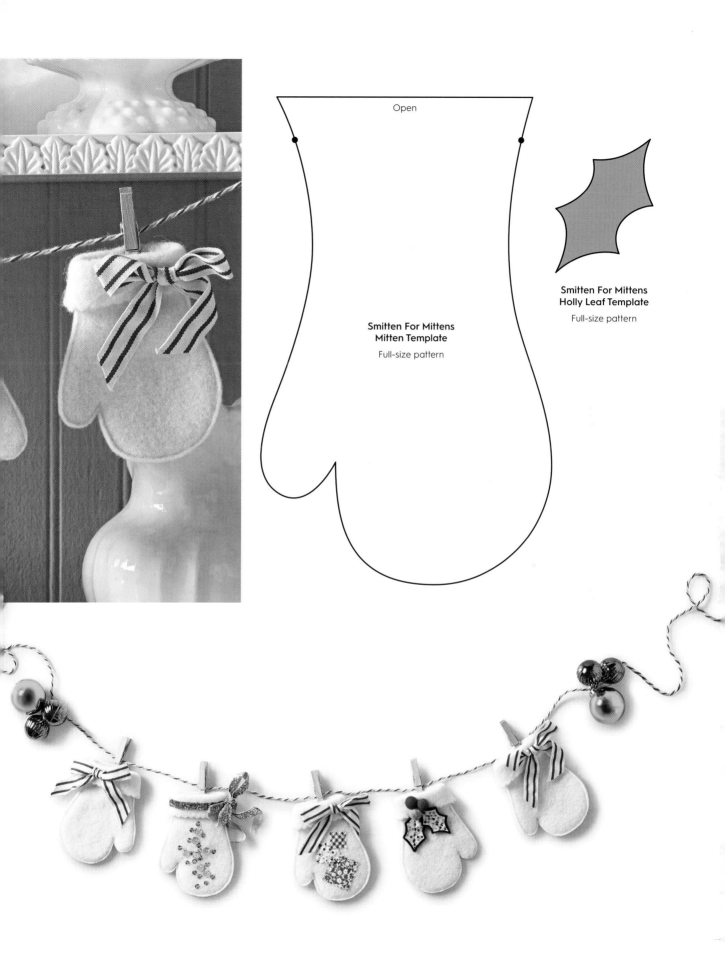

Open

**Smitten For Mittens
Mitten Template**

Full-size pattern

**Smitten For Mittens
Holly Leaf Template**

Full-size pattern

PRETTY IN PINK TABLE SETTING

Vintage dishes, ornaments, and bottle brush trees gather to celebrate favorite collections. A vintage-feel greeting photocopied from a Christmas card tucks between pink Depression glass plates. A vintage brooch serves as a napkin ring.

CERAMIC PASTEL ORNAMENTS

Smooth ceramic shapes turn into subtle trims to decorate your tree for Christmas.

WHAT YOU NEED

Disposable container deep enough to cover height of ornaments • Ceramic ornaments (available at crafts stores) • Acrylic paint in desired colors • Paintbrush • Crafts glue • Fine glitter to match color of ornament • Ribbon or string for hanging

WHAT YOU DO

1. Dip the ornaments in water. Turn upside down and apply a few drops of paint to the bottom of the ornament, letting the paint run down the side of the ornament.

2. To feather the paint, immediately dip back into the water and repeat the process. Let dry.

3. Make fine lines of glue at the tops of the ornaments. Dust with glitter. Add a ribbon or string for hanging.

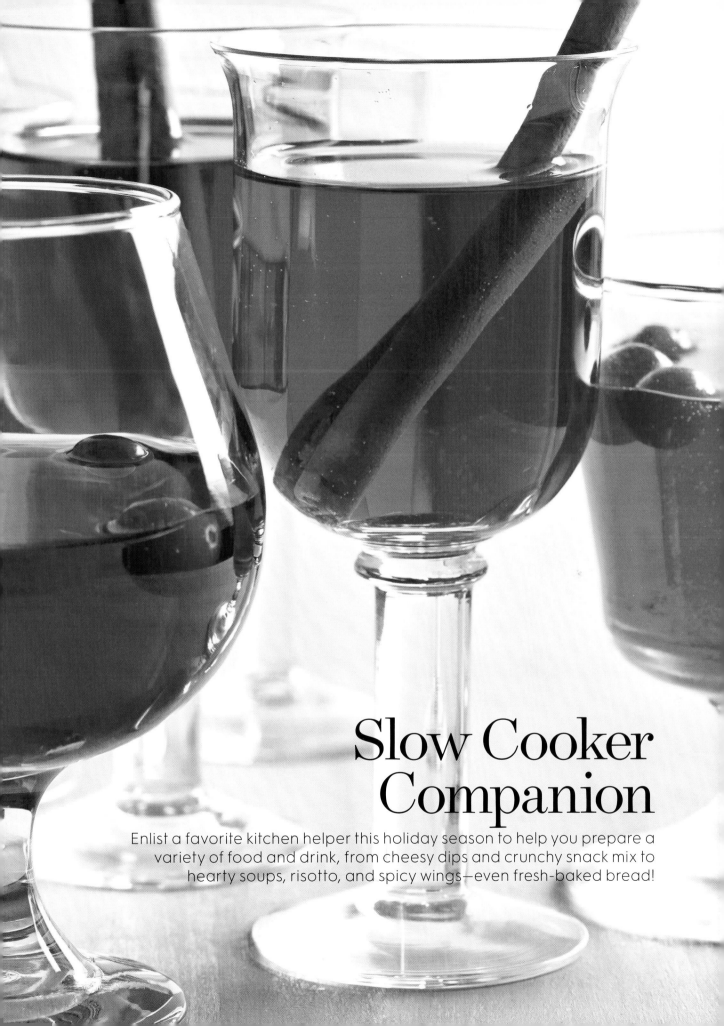

Slow Cooker Companion

Enlist a favorite kitchen helper this holiday season to help you prepare a variety of food and drink, from cheesy dips and crunchy snack mix to hearty soups, risotto, and spicy wings—even fresh-baked bread!

HORCHATA LATTE

The cooling Mexican drink of cinnamon-spiced rice milk is amped up and warmed up for the holidays.

WHAT YOU NEED

7   cups boiling water
3   cups uncooked long grain rice
6   inches stick cinnamon
¾   cup sugar
5   cups vanilla-flavor unsweetened almond milk or rice milk, or reduced-fat milk
3   Tbsp. instant espresso or dark-roast coffee powder
    Ground cinnamon (optional)

WHAT YOU DO

1. In a large pitcher or bowl combine the water, rice, and stick cinnamon. Cover and let stand at room temperature 6 to 24 hours. Remove cinnamon stick.
2. Working in batches, in a blender combine rice mixture and sugar. Cover and blend on high until nearly smooth (mixture will still have bits of rice). Strain through a cheesecloth-lined sieve into a 4-qt. slow cooker. Stir in almond milk and coffee powder.
3. Cover and cook on low 4 hours, whisking once. Whisk well before serving. If desired, sprinkle servings with ground cinnamon. Makes 22 servings.

SCARLET WINE PUNCH

This ruby-red and warm wine punch gets it color from cranberry juice.

WHAT YOU NEED

2   inches stick cinnamon
4   whole cloves
1   32-oz. bottle cranberry juice
⅓   cup packed brown sugar
1   bottle white Zinfandel or dry white wine
    Whole fresh cranberries (optional)
    Stick cinnamon (optional)

WHAT YOU DO

1. For spice bag, cut a double thickness of 100%-cotton cheesecloth into a 6-inch square. Place cinnamon and cloves in the center of the cloth. Bring corners together and tie closed with clean kitchen string. In a 3½- or 4-qt. slow cooker combine spice bag, cranberry juice, and brown sugar.
2. Cover and cook on low 3 to 4 hours or on high 1 to 1½ hours.
3. Remove the spice bag and discard. If using low, turn to high. Stir wine into punch. Cover and cook 30 minutes more. Serve immediately or keep warm, covered, on low up to 2 hours. If desired, top servings with cranberries and/or additional stick cinnamon. Makes 14 servings.

MAKE-IT-MINE
SLOW COOKER PARTY MIX

Believe it or not, you can make perfectly crispy snack mix in your slow cooker. Cooling it in a single layer on a piece of foil or baking pan is key. This mix is about as customizable as it gets. Pick your own cereal, crunchy treat, nuts, and seasonings from an array of options.

WHAT YOU NEED
	Nonstick cooking spray
6	cups Cereal
4	cups Crunchy Treat
3	cups round toasted oat cereal
2½	cups Whole Nuts
¾	cup butter, melted
	Seasonings
3	Tbsp. Worcestershire sauce
	Bottled hot pepper sauce (optional)

WHAT YOU DO
1. Lightly coat an oval 6-qt. slow cooker* with cooking spray. In the prepared cooker combine Cereal, Crunchy Treat, oat cereal, and Whole Nuts.

2. In a small bowl stir together melted butter, Seasonings, Worcestershire sauce, and, if desired, bottled hot pepper sauce. Drizzle butter mixture over cereal mixture; stir gently to coat.

3. Cook, uncovered, on high 1½ hours, stirring from the bottom up every 30 minutes. Turn to low. Cook, uncovered, 20 minutes more or until dry and crisp, stirring from the bottom up every 10 minutes.

4. Spread party mix on a large sheet of foil to cool. Store, covered, at room temperature up to 2 weeks or freeze up to 3 months. Makes 30 servings.

Cereal Sweetened oat square cereal, puffed corn cereal, bite-size corn square cereal, bite-size rice square cereal, bite-size wheat square cereal, crispy corn and rice cereal, and/or toasted high-fiber corn cereal

Crunchy Treat Pretzel sticks, small pretzel twists, bite-size cheese crackers, bagel chips, chow mein noodles, fish-shape crackers, corn chips, and/or oyster crackers

Whole Nuts Mixed nuts, almonds, cashews, pecan halves, walnut halves, peanuts, and/or pumpkin seeds

Seasonings (pick one)

Italian ½ cup grated Parmesan cheese plus 1 tsp. garlic powder. Substitute ¼ cup Italian vinaigrette for the Worcestershire sauce

Ranch One 1-oz. envelope ranch dry salad dressing mix

Cajun 1 tsp. onion powder, 1 tsp. paprika, ¾ tsp. ground white pepper, ¾ tsp. garlic powder, ½ tsp. cayenne pepper, and ¼ tsp. black pepper, plus 1 tsp. hot pepper sauce

Taco One 1-oz. envelope taco seasoning mix plus 1 tsp. ground cumin

*Tip Use an oval slow cooker for best results.

ASIAGO CHEESE DIP

If a cheese dip can be elegant, this is it. Mushrooms, green onions, and dried tomatoes flavor a rich base of sour cream, cream cheese, mayonnaise, and Asiago cheese. Enjoy with crisp slices of toasted French baguette.

WHAT YOU NEED

1   cup chicken broth or water
4   oz. dried tomatoes (not oil-packed)
2   16-oz. cartons light sour cream
1¼ cups light mayonnaise or salad dressing
1   cup finely shredded Asiago cheese
1   cup sliced fresh mushrooms or 1 oz. dried mushrooms
    (porcini, shiitake, chanterelle, and/or oyster),
    coarsely chopped*
1   cup thinly sliced green onions
½   8-oz. pkg. light cream cheese (neufchatel), cut up
    Thinly sliced green onions
    Whole grain baguette-style French bread slices,
    toasted if desired**

WHAT YOU DO

1. In a small saucepan bring broth to boiling. Remove from heat. Add dried tomatoes; cover and let stand 5 minutes. Drain, discarding liquid. Chop tomatoes (about 1¼ cups).
2. Meanwhile, in a 3½- or 4-qt. slow cooker combine sour cream, mayonnaise, Asiago cheese, mushrooms, 1 cup green onions, and cream cheese. Stir in chopped tomatoes.
3. Cover and cook on low 3 to 4 hours or high 1½ to 2 hours. Stir to combine.
4. Serve immediately or keep warm, covered, on warm or low up to 2 hours. Sprinkle with additional green onions and serve with toasted bread slices. Makes 52 servings.
*Tip To rehydrate dried mushrooms, place in a small bowl. Add enough boiling water to cover; let stand 30 minutes. Drain mushrooms, squeezing out any excess liquid. Coarsely chop mushrooms.
**Tip To toast bread slices, preheat broiler. Place bread slices on a large baking sheet. Broil 3 to 4 inches from the heat 2 to 3 minutes or until lightly browned, turning once.

CHEESE FONDUE

Gathering around a pot of bubbly cheese, dipping, and talking is the most social way to eat. The slow cooker ensures perfect results—and the fondue can stay warm on low for the duration of the party (or until it's gone).

WHAT YOU NEED

3   cups reduced-sodium chicken broth
3   cups heavy cream
1   cup dry white wine
3   cloves garlic, minced
½   cup butter, softened
½   cup all-purpose flour
    Seasoning
16 oz. shredded Cheese Option 1

8   oz. shredded or crumbled Cheese Option 2
    French bread cubes, steamed broccoli, boiled
    potatoes, and/or cooked pasta shapes

WHAT YOU DO

1. In a 4- to 5-qt. slow cooker combine broth, cream, wine, and garlic. Cover and cook on low 4 to 5 hours.
2. Meanwhile, in a medium bowl stir together butter and flour until a paste forms. Stir into broth mixture until combined. Cover and cook 30 minutes more or until slightly thickened.
3. Whisk Seasoning into broth mixture. Gradually whisk in Cheese. Serve with French bread cubes, steamed broccoli, boiled potatoes, and/or cooked pasta shapes. Makes 36 servings.
Classic For Seasoning, use 1 Tbsp. Dijon mustard. For Cheese Option 1, use process Swiss. For Cheese Option 2, use shredded Emmentaler.
Cheddar-Beer Prepare as directed, except substitute lager beer for wine. For Seasoning, use 1 Tbsp. spicy brown mustard. For Cheese Option 1, use cheddar. For Cheese Option 2, use shredded sharp cheddar.
Blue For Seasoning, use 2 Tbsp. honey. For Cheese Option 1, use Gruyère. For Cheese Option 2, use crumbled blue cheese.
Chipotle For Seasoning, use 1 to 2 Tbsp. finely chopped canned chipotle peppers in adobo sauce. For Cheese Option 1, use Monterey Jack. For Cheese Option 2, use shredded Colby.
Herbed For Seasoning, use 1 tsp. finely shredded lemon zest. For Cheese Option 1, use Havarti. For Cheese Option 2, use two 5.2-oz. containers semisoft cheese with garlic and fine herbes.
Italian For Seasoning, use 2 Tbsp. basil pesto. For Cheese Option 1, use Italian cheese blend. For Cheese Option 2, use shredded Pecorino Romano.

HOISIN-AND-HONEY CHICKEN WINGS

Serve lots of napkins along with these saucy Asian-inspired wings.

WHAT YOU NEED

16 chicken wings (about 3 lb. total)
½ cup hoisin sauce
¼ cup honey
1 Tbsp. grated fresh ginger
1 Tbsp. toasted sesame oil
4 cloves garlic, minced
   Sesame seeds, toasted
   Sliced green onions

WHAT YOU DO

1. Preheat oven to 375°F. Line a 15×10-inch baking pan with foil. Using a sharp knife, carefully cut off tips of chicken wings; discard wing tips. Cut wings at the joints to make 32 pieces. Place pieces in the prepared baking pan. Bake 20 minutes. Drain off fat.

2. In a 3½- or 4-qt. slow cooker combine hoisin sauce, honey, ginger, sesame oil, and garlic. Add chicken pieces; stir to coat.

3. Cover and cook on low 4 to 5 hours or on high 2 to 2½ hours. Meanwhile, toast sesame seeds in a dry skillet over medium heat 2 minutes or until fragrant and golden, stirring frequently.

4. Serve immediately or keep warm, covered, on warm or low up to 2 hours. Sprinkle with green onions and sesame seeds. Makes 16 servings.

MUSHROOM RISOTTO WITH PEAS

The slow cooker takes the constant stirring out of the risotto equation. This toothsome rice dish can be served as a main course or as a side to roasted chicken or beef.

WHAT YOU NEED

3 Tbsp. butter
3 cups sliced assorted fresh mushrooms, such as button, cremini, and/or shiitake (8 oz.)
⅓ cup sliced shallots or chopped onion
2 cloves garlic, minced
1¾ cups uncooked Arborio rice
4 cups chicken broth
¾ cup dry white wine
½ tsp. cracked black pepper
⅔ cup frozen peas, thawed
   Asiago cheese shards (optional)
   Fresh Italian parsley leaves (optional)

WHAT YOU DO

1. In a large skillet heat butter over medium heat until melted. Add mushrooms, shallots, and garlic; cook 5 to 7 minutes or until mushrooms are lightly browned and liquid is evaporated, stirring occasionally. Stir in rice; cook and stir 1 minute more. Transfer to a 3½- or 4-qt. slow cooker. Stir in broth, wine, and pepper.

2. Cover and cook on low 2¾ hours or on high 1¼ hours or until rice is tender. If possible, remove crockery liner from cooker. Stir in peas. If desired, top with cheese and/or parsley. Makes 8 servings.

GREEK STUFFED MEATBALLS

There's a surprise inside these beef-lamb blend meatballs flavored with olives, parsley, and garlic—a salty bite of feta or Kasseri cheese. The Greek-style tomato sauce is infused with garlic, oregano, red wine, and cinnamon.

WHAT YOU NEED

- 2   eggs, lightly beaten
- 1   cup seasoned fine dry bread crumbs
- ¼   cup finely chopped pimiento-stuffed green olives
- ¼   cup finely chopped black olives
- ¼   cup snipped fresh Italian parsley
- 4   cloves garlic, minced
- 1   tsp. salt
- ¼   tsp. black pepper
- 1   lb. lean ground beef
- 1   lb. ground lamb
- 6   oz. Kasseri or feta cheese, cut into ½-inch cubes
- 1   recipe Greek Tomato Sauce

WHAT YOU DO

1. Preheat oven to 350°F. In a large bowl combine the first eight ingredients (through pepper). Add ground beef and ground lamb; mix well.

2. For each meatball, shape some of the meat mixture into a ball around a cheese cube, being sure to completely enclose cheese. Arrange meatballs in a single layer in a 15×10-inch baking pan. Bake 25 minutes. Drain off fat.

3. Transfer meatballs to a 4- to 5-qt. slow cooker. Pour Greek Tomato Sauce over meatballs; gently toss to coat.

4. Cover and cook on low 3 to 4 hours or on high 1½ to 2 hours. Serve immediately or keep warm, covered, on warm or low up to 2 hours. Makes 42 meatballs.

Greek Tomato Sauce In a medium saucepan cook and stir ½ cup chopped onion and 1 clove minced garlic in 1 Tbsp. olive oil over medium heat until onion is tender. Stir in one 8-oz. can tomato sauce; ¼ cup dry red wine or beef broth; 1 tsp. dried oregano, crushed; and ½ tsp. ground cinnamon; heat through.

3. Add onions, carrots, and celery to the reserved drippings. Cook and stir over medium heat 10 to 15 minutes or until tender. Add mustard, garlic, and herbes de Provence. Cook and stir 2 minutes more. Transfer to the cooker. Stir in tomatoes, broth, and wine.

4. Cover and cook on low 8 to 10 hours. Using a slotted spoon, transfer ribs and vegetables to a serving platter; cover with foil to keep warm.

5. For sauce, skim fat from cooking liquid in cooker; measure 3 cups and discard the remaining liquid. In a medium saucepan combine the 3 cups reserved liquid and cornstarch. Cook and stir over medium-high heat until mixture is slightly thickened and bubbly. Cook and stir 2 minutes more. Season to taste with additional salt and pepper.

6. Spoon sauce over ribs and vegetables.* If desired, serve with Rich Mashed Potatoes. Makes 10 servings.

*Tip If desired, return ribs and vegetables to the cooker. Pour sauce over ribs and vegetables. Keep warm, covered, on warm or low up to 1 hour before serving.

Rich Mashed Potatoes Peel and quarter 3 lb. potatoes. In a Dutch oven cook potatoes, covered, in enough boiling salted water to cover 20 to 25 minutes or until tender; drain. In a large bowl beat potatoes with a mixer on medium until light and fluffy. Add 4 oz. softened cream cheese, ½ cup sour cream, and 2 Tbsp. softened butter. Beat on low just until combined. Stir in 1 cup finely shredded Swiss cheese.

GARAM MASALA CHICKEN STEW WITH PEAS AND POTATOES

Garam masala is an Indian (not hot) blend of both sweet (such as cinnamon) and savory (such as cumin) spices.

WHAT YOU NEED
- Nonstick cooking spray
- 6 large skinless, boneless chicken thighs (about 1½ lb. total)
- 2 medium red-skin potatoes, cut into ½-inch cubes
- 1 medium onion, thinly sliced
- 1½ tsp. grated fresh ginger
- 2 cloves garlic, minced
- ½ tsp. salt
- ½ tsp. black pepper
- 1 14.5-oz. can reduced-sodium chicken broth
- 1 8-oz. can no-salt-added tomato sauce
- 1 cup frozen peas
- ½ cup plain fat-free yogurt
- 2 tsp. garam masala

WHAT YOU DO
1. Lightly coat a large skillet with cooking spray; heat skillet over medium-high heat. Add chicken; cook 6 minutes or until browned on both sides. Drain off fat.

2. In a 3½- or 4-qt. slow cooker combine potatoes, onion, ginger, and garlic. Top with chicken. Sprinkle with salt and pepper. Pour broth and tomato sauce over mixture in cooker.

3. Cover and cook on low 5½ hours or on high 2¾ hours. If using low turn to high. Stir in frozen peas, yogurt, and garam masala. Cover and cook 15 minutes more. Makes 6 servings.

BEAUJOLAIS-BRAISED BEEF SHORT RIBS

The slow cooker provides the ideal environment and method—moist, prolonged cooking—for turning this tough cut into tender, fall-off-the-bone ribs. Serve it with Rich Mashed Potatoes—or a creamy polenta if you like.

WHAT YOU NEED
- 6 lb. beef short ribs
- ½ cup all-purpose flour
- ½ tsp. salt
- ¼ tsp. black pepper
- ⅓ cup olive oil
- 2 cups chopped onions
- 1 cup chopped carrots
- ½ cup chopped celery
- 3 Tbsp. stone-ground Dijon mustard
- 8 cloves garlic, halved
- 1 tsp. dried herbes de Provence, crushed
- 1 14.5-oz. can diced tomatoes, undrained
- 1 cup lower-sodium beef broth
- 1 cup Beaujolais or other fruity red wine
- 2 Tbsp. cornstarch
- 1 recipe Rich Mashed Potatoes (optional)

WHAT YOU DO
1. Trim fat from short ribs. In a plastic bag combine flour, salt, and pepper. Add a few ribs at a time; shake to coat.

2. In a large skillet heat oil over medium-high heat. Working in batches, cook ribs in hot oil until browned on all sides. Transfer ribs to a 6-qt. slow cooker. Drain off fat, reserving 2 Tbsp. drippings in skillet.

DANISH GREEN KALE SOUP

A handful of quick-cooking oats thickens and gives body to this super-healthful soup.

WHAT YOU NEED

1	recipe Ham Broth or 10 cups chicken broth
1½	lb. potatoes, peeled and cubed
2	cups cubed cooked ham or coarsely chopped meat from pork hocks
1½	cups sliced carrots
1	cup chopped leeks
1	cup sliced celery
3	cloves garlic, minced
½	tsp. grated whole nutmeg
½	tsp. black pepper
¾	cup quick-cooking rolled oats
4	cups coarsely chopped, trimmed fresh kale
1	Tbsp. snipped fresh thyme

WHAT YOU DO

1. In a 5- to 6-qt. slow cooker combine the first nine ingredients (through pepper).

2. Cover and cook on low 8 to 10 hours or on high 4 to 5 hours.

3. If cooking on low, turn to high. Gradually stir in oats. Stir in kale and thyme. Cover and cook 30 minutes more. Makes 8 servings.

Ham Broth In a 6-qt. slow cooker combine 10 cups water; 2 lb. meaty smoked pork hocks; 3 stalks celery, cut up; 2 medium carrots, cut up; 1 medium onion, halved; ¼ cup loosely packed fresh thyme sprigs; 3 bay leaves; and 3 cloves garlic, minced. Cover and cook on high 4 to 6 hours. Remove pork hocks. Cut meat off bones; coarsely chop meat and discard bones. Line a large sieve with a double thickness of 100%-cotton cheesecloth; strain broth through sieve. Discard solids. Cover and chill broth and meat separately until ready to use. Before using, lift fat off broth. If necessary, add enough water to broth to measure 10 cups.

ROSEMARY-PARMESAN BREAD WITH GARLIC BUTTER

Yes, you can make bread in your slow cooker! A quick broil after it comes out of the cooker crisps the crust.

WHAT YOU NEED

1½	cups warm water (105°F to 115°F)
1	pkg. active dry yeast
2⅔	cups all-purpose flour
3	Tbsp. whole wheat flour
⅓	cup finely shredded Parmesan cheese
1	Tbsp. finely snipped fresh rosemary
1½	tsp. salt
	Nonstick cooking spray
1	Tbsp. yellow cornmeal
2	Tbsp. butter, melted
¼	tsp. garlic salt

WHAT YOU DO

1. In an extra-large bowl stir together the warm water and yeast; let stand 10 minutes or until mixture is foamy. Add flours, cheese, rosemary, and salt to yeast mixture; stir just until combined. Stir 1 minute more or until dough forms a ball. (Dough will be very soft and sticky.) Cover bowl with plastic wrap; let stand at room temperature 2 hours.

2. Lightly coat a 5- to 6-qt. slow cooker with cooking spray. Line the bottom of the cooker with parchment paper; coat paper with cooking spray and sprinkle with cornmeal. Turn dough out onto a well-floured surface; shape into a ball. Place in the center of the prepared cooker.

3. Cover and cook on high 2 hours or until an instant-read thermometer inserted near the center registers 200°F, giving the crockery liner a half-turn halfway through cooking if possible. (Do not lift the lid.)

4. Preheat broiler. Remove bread from cooker; peel off parchment paper. Place bread on an ungreased baking sheet. Broil 4 to 6 inches from the heat 3 to 4 minutes or until bread is golden and surface is no longer moist. Transfer to a wire rack. Brush with melted butter; sprinkle with garlic salt. Cool completely before slicing. Makes 16 servings.

Let Heaven and Nature Sing

Turn to nature for the perfect inspiration to make your holiday sing with all that brings joy to the world.

NATURAL LOG CANDLES

WHAT YOU NEED

Large limb or logs cut into 6- to 10-inch lengths • Drill and drill bit large enough to accommodate tea light • Tea light candles in metal holders • Twine in desired colors • Acorns • Acrylic paint in desired colors • Paintbrush • Scissors

WHAT YOU DO

1. Use the drill and drill bit to drill a hole large enough to accommodate the tea light candle.

2. Paint the acorn bottoms with desired color of paint. Let dry. Set aside.

3. Wrap the wood pieces with twine and tie in place. Use another piece of twine to tie the acorns to the sides of the wood pieces.

4. Place the tea light candle in the holes of the wood.

Never leave a burning candle unattended.

JOY TO THE WORLD TREE FAVORS

Little slices of wood stack up to make joyful favors for your holiday table.

WHAT YOU NEED

Wood slices in various sizes (available at crafts stores or online) • Awl • Hot-glue gun and glue sticks • Crafts glue • Vintage music or copyright-free music • Tiny sticks • Gold glitter

WHAT YOU DO

1. Place the slices of wood atop one another to resemble a tree. Set aside.

2. Use an awl to make a small hole on the top piece of wood. Glue the wood slices together using little dabs of hot glue.

3. Tear little strips of the music and glue to the edges of the wood as desired using crafts glue.

4. Using hot glue, glue the tiny sticks together to form a star. Paint with crafts glue and dust with glitter. Let dry. Glue into the hole on the top of the tree using hot glue.

BANNER DAY

Let motifs from nature inspire you to make a banner that celebrates the season. Cut out trees and stars from ivory felt and stitch to a neutral burlap background for a natural look.

WHAT YOU NEED

½ yard natural burlap • Scissors • Ivory felt • Water-soluble marking pen • Brown embroidery floss • 1½ yards of metallic gold cording • ½-inch-wide sheer ivory ribbon • Ivory sewing thread

WHAT YOU DO

1. Cut five 5×11-inch pieces from burlap. Pull threads to create ½ -inch-long fringe on all edges of each piece. Fold each piece in half to measure 5×5½ inches; press.

2. Enlarge and trace patterns, right, onto white paper; cut out. Using a water-soluble marking pen, trace 3 trees and 2 stars onto ivory felt; cut out. Lay out burlap pieces with folded edge at top. Center a felt star or tree on each burlap piece. Use brown embroidery floss to stitch short even-length running stitches around edges of each felt piece, stitching through felt and top burlap layer.

3. Lay cording flat. Sandwich cording between the layers of each burlap piece, alternating motifs. Adjust pieces so cording lies flat against folded edges.

4. Cut ten 3½-inch lengths of sheer ivory ribbon. Use ivory thread to topstitch a ribbon 1 inch below the folded edge on each burlap piece, stitching through both burlap layers and keeping cording free of stitches. Topstitch a second ribbon just above bottom fringe on each burlap piece. Tie a loop at each cording end.

Banner Day Templates

Enlarge 150%

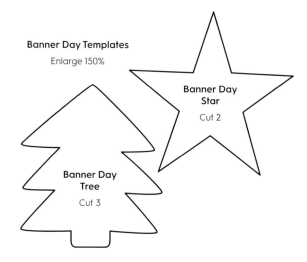

Banner Day Star

Cut 2

Banner Day Tree

Cut 3

TAG ALONG

Build these snowmen without the frigid temps and add them to tags for your holiday packages. There's no snow involved, just narrow paper strips rolled tightly into circles using a quilling tool.

WHAT YOU NEED

12-inch lengths of ⅛-inch-wide white and black quilling paper strips • Paper crimping tool (optional) • Quilling tool • Crafts glue • Brown kraft paper tags • White glitter • Silver cord or bakers twine

WHAT YOU DO

1. Crimp white paper strips with crimping tool if desired. Using a quilling tool, roll a strip into a tight circle. (For larger circles, glue strips end to end before rolling.) Glue strip end to the circle with a dot of glue. Use 1 or 2 white paper strips for the snowman head, 2 or 3 white paper strips for the middle, and 3 or 4 white paper strips for the bottom.

2. Cut 2 black paper strips each 3 to 6 inches long. Roll each strip into a tight circle to make a button.

3. Roll a 12-inch-long black paper strip into a tight circle. Pinch the circle into a square shape for the hat. Cut a 1-inch-long black paper strip and fold it crosswise in half for the hat brim.

4. Glue the snowman head, middle, and bottom to a kraft paper tag. To give the body more dimension, push the centers of the middle and bottom circles out slightly; glue to secure. Place glue on each button and push it into the center of the snowman middle or bottom, or place it sideways on top of the coils; let dry.

5. Glue the brim and hat to the top of the snowman head. Brush a light coat of crafts glue on snowman and its edges and dot glue on tag around snowman; sprinkle white glitter on wet glue.

6. Thread silver cord or bakers twine through tag hole for a hanger.

WRAPPED ACORNS

Natural acorns are wrapped with sky-blue fibers to make a tiny grouping for your door or tie-ons for special packages.

WHAT YOU NEED

Natural acorns • Crafts glue • Paintbrush • Bakers twine or pearl cotton thread • Drill and ⅛-inch drill bit (optional) • Scissors

WHAT YOU DO

1. Be sure the acorns are clean and dry. Starting at the bottom of the acorn, brush the glue onto the acorn and wrap the twine or cotton thread around the acorn, stopping at the acorn top. Let dry.

2. Use the drill and bit to make a tiny hole at the base of the stem of the acorn or tie a piece of twine around the top.

3. Group the acorns for hanging or attaching to a package.

GALAXY GARLAND

Felt stars align atop one another to create a garland to adorn any mantel, tree, or shelf. There is no limit to the number of stars you can create.

WHAT YOU NEED

Nonwoven felt such as National Nonwovens in blues and grays • Plain and printed buttons in various sizes • 3- to 4-foot length of ⅜-inch gray grosgrain ribbon • Scissors • Needle • Matching thread

WHAT YOU DO

1. Trace the pattern templates, page 135, and cut out from desired colors of felt. Cut enough stars to stack the stars as desired.

2. Stack the stars as desired with the ribbon running between the stack of stars. Tack in place using needle and thread.

3. Sew the buttons on both sides of the felt stars using matching thread.

4. Trim the ends of the ribbon.

**Galaxy Garland
Star Templates**

Full-size patterns

Wood slices are drilled and then strung with natural-color fibers to create star-inspired trims for holiday decorating.

WOOD SLICE STAR ORNAMENTS

Slices of wood are drilled and strung with yarn to make nature-inspired stars for your holiday tree.

WHAT YOU NEED

Wood slices (available at crafts stores or make yourself)
• Pencil • Drill and drill bit • Yarn in natural colors • Needle large enough to accommodate yarn • String

WHAT YOU DO

1. Drill a hole in the center of log slice and 8 holes around the outside of the log slice, alternating lengths to create a star shape, adjusting for the size of your log slice. Drill a hole to attach a string for hanging at the top.

2. Thread the needle with the yarn. Starting in the center of the log slice, stitch from the center to a hole on the outside. Work your way around the outside until all holes have been stitched. Tie loose ends together in the back of the log slice.

3. Attach a string in the top hole for hanging.

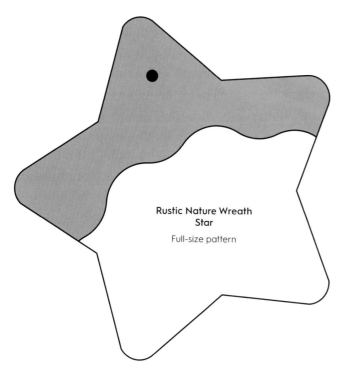

**Rustic Nature Wreath
Star**

Full-size pattern

RUSTIC NATURE WREATH

Sticks and stars combine to make a welcoming square-shaped wreath for your holiday entrance. Stars are adorned with winter-white doilies and dusted with snowy glitter. A vintage reindeer perches on the wreath.

WHAT YOU NEED

• Sticks of different lengths • Hot-glue gun and glue sticks
• Thin wood stars (available at crafts stores) or thin wood to cut your own and saw • White paper doilies • White glitter •
Crafts glue • Scissors • Fresh or artificial greenery • Twine •
Small vintage reindeer figure (optional)

WHAT YOU DO

1. Plan the design of the wreath by laying the sticks on a flat surface, overlapping and breaking or cutting the sticks until the desired look is achieved. Glue in place using hot glue.
2. Use twine to wrap around the middle and ends of the wreath.
3. If making your own wood stars, trace chosen pattern, left, and cut out star with hand or band saw. Cut pieces of the doily and glue to the wood star shapes. Run a bead of glue on top and edge of the doily and dust with white glitter. Let dry.
4. Tie the stars onto the string and tie onto the wreath.
5. Tuck bits of greenery between the sticks. Attach vintage reindeer if desired.
6. Add a piece of twine at the top for hanging.

NATURE FINDING WREATH

Take a nature walk and gather findings to create a stunning wreath that will last year after year.

WHAT YOU NEED

• Items from nature such as acorns, small pinecones, and sticks • Small wood slices (available at crafts stores or make yourself) • Hot-glue gun and glue sticks • Wood picture frame • Ribbon

WHAT YOU DO

1. Plan the design of the wreath by laying out all of the natural elements. Beginning at one corner of the frames, use hot glue to glue each of the items to the frame, filling in with small items. Let glue dry completely before moving.
2. Loop a ribbon through the top of the wreath. Tie a bow and attach at the top of the wreath with hot glue.

WOOD SLICE NAPKIN HOLDERS

Wood slices woodburned with a holiday motif become one-of-a-kind napkin rings.

WHAT YOU NEED

Wood slices (available at crafts stores or make yourself) • Pencil • Woodburning tool • Twine • Hot-glue gun and glue sticks • Napkin • Fresh greenery

WHAT YOU DO

1. Plan the design of the motif or refer to the design inspiration in photos, above. Use a pencil to mark designs if desired. Using the woodburning tool, burn the design into the front of the wood slice.
2. Make a loop using the twine. Glue to the back of the wood slice. Slide the napkin through the loop and tuck in fresh greenery.

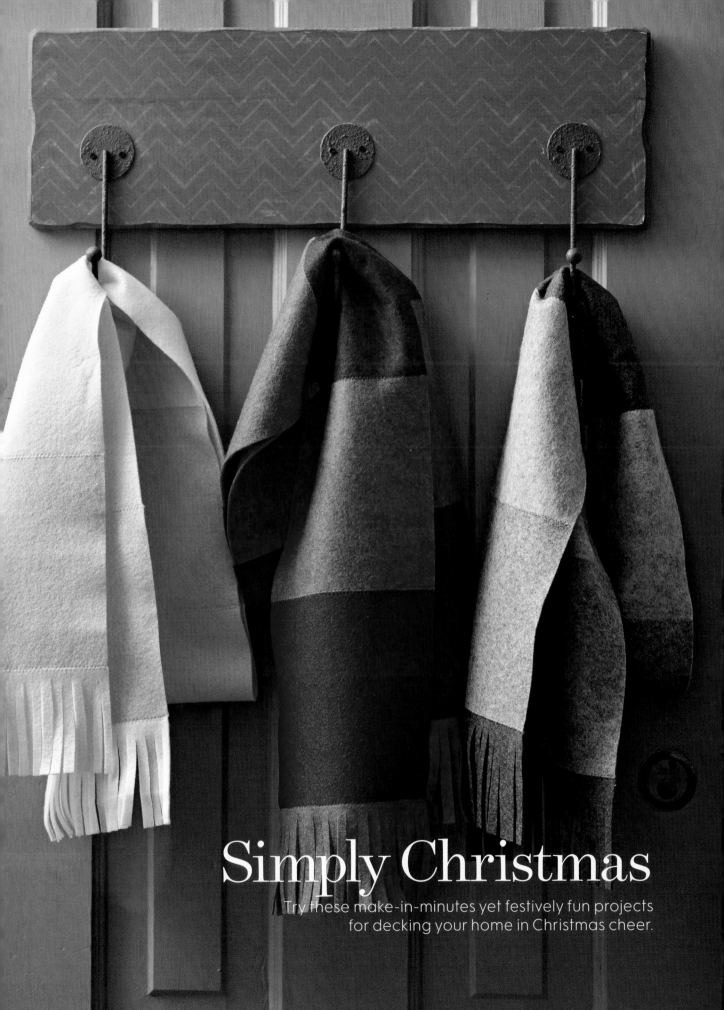

Simply Christmas

Try these make-in-minutes yet festively fun projects for decking your home in Christmas cheer.

APPLE CANDLES

Granny Smith apples become clever candleholders when they are displayed with taper candles in a vintage muffin tin.

WHAT YOU NEED

Muffin tin • Granny Smith apples • Knife • Taper candles

WHAT YOU DO

1. Set the muffin tin on a flat surface. Choose apples that fit into the tin.
2. Remove the stems of the apples. Use the knife to cut a hole at the top of each apple.
3. Place a candle in each hole, cutting the candle shorter if needed. Adjust the candles. Place apples and candles in tin.

Never leave a burning candle unattended.

SIMPLY-STATED GREETING

Purchased letters can spell any greeting you want to share when you paint and adorn them with simple stickers.

WHAT YOU NEED

Wood letters in desired style (available at crafts stores) • Red acrylic paint • Paintbrush • 3-D stickers

WHAT YOU NEED

1. Be sure the wood letters are clean and dry. Paint with red paint. Let dry.
2. Attach 3-D stickers onto the letters and display on a mantel, window ledge, or in a wreath.

Soft and subtle nonwoven felt comes in dozens and dozens of rich and beautiful colors. Choose the color palette that suits your fancy and create scarves for everyone on your Christmas list.

BEAUTIFULLY SIMPLE FELT SCARVES

Choose your favorite colors of nonwoven felt to make these simple yet stunning scarves for gifts or to wear to holiday parties.

WHAT YOU NEED

Nonwoven felt such as National Nonwovens in desired colors • Scissors • Invisible thread • Sewing machine • Iron (optional)

WHAT YOU DO

1. Plan the design and color pattern of the scarf by choosing at least 3 colors of felt. Cut the felt pieces into 6½×6½-inch squares. Cut a 6½×3¼-inch rectangle for each end for the fringe. Cut approximately 9 squares, depending on desired length of the scarf.

2. Butt the edges up to each other and use the sewing machine and invisible thread to stitch them together using a small zigzag stitch. Press if necessary.

3. Fringe the last rectangle on each side by cutting 3-inch-long slits ⅜ inch apart. Press if desired.

EASY CROSS-STITCH KITCHEN TOWEL

Simple cross-stitches line up to form a familiar motif on a purchased kitchen towel.

WHAT YOU NEED

Purchased cotton kitchen dish towel • Transfer paper (optional) • Washable fabric pencil • Green embroidery floss in desired colors • Embroidery needle • Embroidery hoop (optional) • Scissors

WHAT YOU DO

1. Wash, dry, and iron the towel. Referring to the template pattern, left, plan the placement of the design on the towel.
2. Transfer the design to the towel or mark with a pencil where you want the stitches.
3. Thread the need with 3 strands of embroidery floss and use cross-stitches to make the design. Clip any threads on the back. Press the finished towel.

SPARKLING POINSETTIA
A vintage wood box filled with a poinsettia lights up for the holidays for easy holiday decor.

WHAT YOU NEED
Vintage wood box • Small plastic lid or foil for bottom of box • 2 small poinsettias in desired colors • Battery-operated lights

WHAT YOU DO
1. Be sure the box is clean and dry. Place a plastic lid or foil in the bottom of the box.
2. Put the poinsettias in the box, arranging to fit. Tuck the lights into the poinsettias.

PINECONE NAPKIN RINGS

Paint a pinecone with silver paint and tie it with ribbon and found sticks onto a neutral-tone napkin for a stunning and simple table favor.

Pinecones of all sizes and shapes become the center of easy diy projects for quick holiday decorating.

PINECONES IN A TRAY

Choose a favorite tray and fill it with painted pinecones to set at an entrance or to use as a simple centerpiece.

PINECONES IN GLASS

Purchased clear glass or plastic ornaments with removable tops showcase little pinecones and other findings of nature's bounty. Simply remove the top of the ornament, fill with nature items, and replace the ornament top.

SWITCH-IT-UP STOCKINGS

Purchased stockings make it easy to personalize each one for Santa to fill this year.

WHAT YOU NEED

Purchased stocking in plain color • Iron (optional) • Trims such as pom-pom trim, burlap ribbon, buttons, etc. • Fabric glue • Scissors • Needle • Thread to match stocking and trims

WHAT YOU DO

1. Press the stocking if necessary. Plan the design of the stocking by laying the trims on the stocking. Try placing some of the trims tucked under the cuff and placing some on the heel and toe.

2. Glue the trims in place. Sew on button if using.

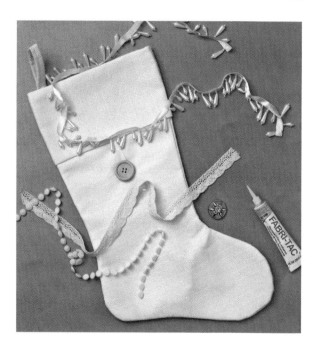

LET IT SNOW TAGS

Simply made gift tags are created using punched snowflakes atop pretty paper doilies. Make them by the dozens—no two will be alike.

WHAT YOU NEED

4-inch-diameter paper doily • Manila tag • Crafts glue • Red cardstock • Snowflake punch or die-cutting tool with snowflake cartridge • Pop dot • Red-and-white bakers twine

WHAT YOU DO

1. Lay paper doily facedown on work surface and lay tag on top so a rounded doily edge overlaps a portion of the tag; cut doily piece to fit portion of the tag. Glue doily piece to tag.
2. Punch or cut a snowflake from red cardstock. Adhere snowflake to doily on tag with a pop dot.
3. Fold a length of bakers twine in half and thread the fold through the hole in the tag. Thread ends through the folded end and pull to tighten.

WRAPPED IN RIBBON

Holiday-theme cookie cutters are the secret ingredients for making these clever ornaments.

WHAT YOU NEED

⅜-inch-wide red-and-white gingham ribbon • Small star-, tree-, or bell-shape metal cookie cutter • Crafts glue • Red-and-white bakers twine

WHAT YOU DO

1. Unwind ribbon from spool. Place one end of ribbon against the inside of a cookie cutter and wrap the ribbon around the end several times to secure it. Continue wrapping ribbon around the cookie cutter, slightly overlapping wraps until all sides of the cookie cutter are covered. Secure the end of ribbon with crafts glue.
2. Thread a short length of bakers twine through the ornament; tie the ends to form a hanging loop.

BRIGHT AND BOLD TIED FELT GARLAND

Little snippets of colorful felt tie together with felt beads to make a festive garland.

WHAT YOU NEED

Small strips (about 1×5 inches) of nonwoven felt such as National Nonwovens in desired colors • Felt balls in desired colors and sizes • String • Needle to accommodate string

WHAT YOU DO

1. Plan the design by laying out the strips of colored felt and the felt balls.
2. Using the needle, thread the balls onto the string, leaving space between to tie the strips. Tie the strips between the balls. Trim the ends.

SMOOTH AS VELVET NAPKIN RINGS

How about a little formal wear for your holiday table? Bow-tie napkin rings will dress it up!

WHAT YOU NEED

1½-inch-wide velvet ribbon • Hot-glue gun and glue sticks

WHAT YOU DO

1. For napkin ring, cut a 3-inch piece of ribbon, form loop, and hot-glue ends together.
2. For bow tie, cut 8 inches of ribbon, form loop, flatten, and hot-glue ends together. Cut a little more than 3 inches of ribbon (to allow for slight overlap) for center of bow tie. Pinch flattened loop loosely in middle, wrap cut ribbon around it, and hot-glue ends together in back. Hot-glue bow tie to napkin ring.

QUICK-AS-A-WINK CANDLE IDEAS

Make a simple centerpiece using a candle, a container, and some found-around-the-house accents.

SPARKLING JINGLE BELL CANDLE

Choose a white dish and a white candle. Place the candle in the dish and surround with metallic and white jingle bells.

ALL-IN-RED CRANBERRY CANDLE

Choose a red dish or colander. Place a red candle in the middle and surround with fresh cranberries.

CITRUS CANDLE

Choose a long glass dish and an orange candle. Place the candle in the dish and surround with cut oranges.

Never leave a burning candle unattended.

INDEX

STITCH DIAGRAMS

Backstitch

Straight Stitch

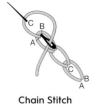

Chain Stitch

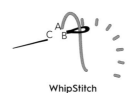

WhipStitch

French Knot

Buttonhole Stitch

Running Stitch

Fern Stitch

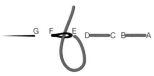

Star Stitch

Stem Stitch

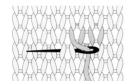

Duplicate Stitch

SOURCES

Paint:
deltacreative.com
plaidonline.com

Paper/Scrapbooking Supplies:
hobbylobby.com
michaels.com

Paper tape/ribbon:
cutetape.com

Acrylic Paint:
deltacreative.com
plaidonline.com

Spray Paint:
walmart.com
menards.com

Wood Slices:
michaels.com

Felt:
National Nonwovens
nationalnonwovens.com

Glue:
Aleene's Tacky Glue
aleenes.com

Beads:
michaels.com
joann.com

Papers and Stickers:
Memory Bound Scrapbook
    Store, Ankeny, Iowa
    memoryboundscrapbook
    store.com
michaels.com
hobbylobby.com

Bakers twine:
hobbylobby.com

Felt balls:
amazon.com

Ribbon:
offray.com

Velvet ribbon:
mjtrim.com
    New York, New York

CRAFT DESIGNERS

Judy Bailey • Lindsay Berger • Jan Carlson • Lisa and Sarah Cox • Carol Field Dahlstrom • Roger Dahlstrom • Michelle Down • Michelle Edwards • Becky Lau Ekstrand • Pam Koelling • Matthew Mead • Susan Parsons • Janet Pittman • Olga Sazonava • Amy Sinibaldi • Suzonne Stirling • Jan Temeyer • LeeAnn Williams